Fr Thomas Crean O.P.

THE MASS
and the
SAINTS

FAMILY PUBLICATIONS • OXFORD

© Family Publications 2008

All rights reserved

ISBN 978-1871217-77-3

Pictures courtesy of Br Lawrence Lew O.P.

published by
Family Publications
Denis Riches House, 66 Sandford Lane
Kennington, Oxford OX1 5RP
www.familypublications.co.uk

Printed in England by
Cromwell Press, Trowbridge, Wilts.

CONTENTS

INTRODUCTION

St Thomas Aquinas tells us that since the Fall, men have had to receive God's grace through material things.[1] Our first father enjoyed an immediate communion with God, and could raise his mind without difficulty to his Creator. We cannot: our thoughts remain for the most part among the things that we sense or remember or imagine. So God, bending down towards us, has taken some of these things and uses them to bring us back to him.

The Church holds that of all the material things which may lead us to God, the most powerful are the seven sacraments, of which the greatest is known to be the Holy Eucharist. Again, that the sacraments may achieve their full effect, the Church clothes them in a rite corresponding to their power. We can therefore expect that the rite of the sacrament of the Holy Eucharist will be calculated, beyond all other visible and audible things, to draw us from ourselves to God. Likewise, since this sacrament contains not only the power of grace but also the author of grace, we can expect its rite to exceed in splendour that of all the other sacraments.

We who believe that bread, when duly consecrated, becomes Christ's body, hold that this consecration may by no means be done except by those noble ceremonies

---

1. *Summa Theologiae* 3a Q. LXI, a. 1.

of the Mass, without which it were unworthy that so great a sacrament be confected.[2]

*   *   *

Sacred Scripture has both a literal and a mystical sense. The literal sense is that expressed by the words themselves and intended by their human author. The mystical sense is that which God has placed within it, and has signified by the events that the words record. Thus we have it on the authority of St Peter that the Flood of Noah, described in the Book of Genesis, was not only a real flood destroying all mortal things, but also a figure of Baptism by which every sin is washed from the soul.

That something similar is true of the Mass is a recurring theme in the tradition of the Church. The Mass possesses both a literal and a mystical sense. It is both the offering of Christ's body and blood, to God the Father then to the faithful, and a memorial of all God's dealing with mankind since the Fall. As St Thomas says, 'This sacrament embraces the entire mystery of our salvation.'[3] And the psalmist sings, 'He hath made a remembrance of his wonderful works; he hath given food to them that fear him' (Ps. 110:4). So a literal interpretation of the Mass explains how its words and gestures are directed towards the sacrifice and communion that occur here and now. A mystical interpretation sets forth the Mass as a memorial of God's wonderful works, and in particular of what

---

2. St John Fisher, *Against Oecolampadius*, Bk. III, c. 1.
3. 3a Q. LXXXIII, a. 4.

pertains to the incarnate Son. The literal sense must have been intended by those, apostles or bishops, who first employed the words and gestures which express it. The mystical sense need not have been intended by them, but may have been placed within their words and gestures by the Holy Spirit, to be uncovered by later generations.

It is true that the Church's rites are not necessarily inspired in the same sense as holy Scripture. Of Scripture we must hold not only that it contains revelation without admixture of error, but also that God is truly the author of all its parts.[4] The Church has not taught the same concerning the liturgy. Though there can be nothing displeasing to God in a liturgical rite duly approved by the supreme authority of the Church, it need not proceed so immediately from him as the words of the prophets and apostles. A sign of this is that whilst all Catholics possess the same Scriptures, all do not worship the Holy Trinity in the same way. Yet it is reasonable to suppose that divine providence, to which nothing can be unimportant, has watched with an especial care over the formation of the sacred liturgy, and above all, of the rite of Mass. If the holy sacrifice is that on earth which is most precious to God, he has surely willed it to be clothed in those forms that will make it so to his children also. And if the worship of the Old Testament was divinely ordained in precise detail,[5] why should not the details of the New Testament

---

4. Cf. Vatican I, Constitution *Dei Filius*.
5. Exodus 25–30.

worship also be filled with meaning, by the providence of God?

I have spoken, in accord with tradition, of the literal and mystical meaning of the Mass. Yet at the heart of the Mass, the Canon, these two senses merge. For the Passion of Christ is not only symbolised by the ceremonial of the altar, but also perpetuated upon it in sacramental form. The separate consecration of Host and Chalice does not only recall the separation of Christ's body and blood; it effects it, insofar as this may now be done. And the other mysteries of his life, though not perpetuated in the same way, are symbolised in the Mass not only as past or future, but also as present: present to God. I believe that this is what the mystical commentators mean when they say, for example, that the *Gloria* signifies Christ's birth, or the commingling his resurrection. God wills that the Mass be the expression in time of his Son's glorious deeds, present to his eternity.

The spiritual sense of Scripture, of course, is itself manifold. Moreover, 'The true body of Christ, and the things done in it, are figures of the mystical body of Christ, and the things done in that.'[6] So we should not be surprised to find that some writers have understood the Mass as a recapitulation not only of the earthly life of the Word incarnate, but also of the earthly pilgrimage of his Church. In this way, the same ceremony may receive more than one spiritual interpretation. 'One mystical explanation does not exclude another', said

---

6. St Thomas Aquinas, *Quodlibetal Questions*, VII, VI, a.2.

Pope Benedict XIV in his classic commentary on the
Roman rite.[7]

★　　　★　　　★

In the present work, I have brought together passages
from writers of all the centuries in which the Mass
has been offered, to provide a continuous commentary
on this pre-eminent action. Most of the authors are
canonised or beatified saints of the Church, and many
are doctors of the Church. Some others have had their
causes of beatification opened. A few have not been
raised to the altars, and perhaps never will be: but their
antiquity and the esteem in which their works have been
held in the Church seemed to justify their inclusion. On
the other hand, I have tried not to multiply less familiar
names: so on several occasions, I have quoted from
Durandus, even when he is repeating an interpretation
found in some earlier author. In two places I have made
bold to suggest an interpretation of my own; these are
indicated by the word, 'Gloss'.

Many of the translations are my own. I have not
given references, except in a general way at the end.
Sometimes I have adjusted a conjunction or omitted
a word or phrase, without significantly changing the
meaning, in order to make the whole run more smoothly.
Occasionally I have brought quotations from different
parts of an author's writings and joined them together
to bring out his whole thought on some question.[8]

---

7. *De Sanctissimo Sacrificio Missae,* Bk II, c. X, 19: *Mysticarum explicationum
altera alteram non excludit.*
8. For example, St Robert Bellarmine's thoughts on liturgical language and
St Thomas Aquinas' on those for whom Mass may be offered.

None of this would be acceptable if this work were offered as a contribution to scholarship. But since it is meant simply as an aid to meditation and devotion, I hope that no one will protest.

*   *   *

It may be asked why I have arranged this catena as a commentary on the *usus antiquior* of the Roman rite, and not on the Mass of Pope Paul VI. The simple answer is that the great bulk of quotations in this work are drawn from priests who offered Mass according to the *usus antiquior*, or in some very similar way. It seemed reasonable to attach their commentaries to the Ordo to which they directly correspond (I have also included a few references to perennial details of the Roman rite which are, however, not found in the liturgical books promulgated under Blessed John XXIII.)

Nevertheless, I believe that whatever the form of Mass at which someone assists, these quotations may prove inspiring. A few may be controversial in our day, for example some of those referring to liturgical language. But I hope that none will be thought unworthy of consideration.

For those who are unfamiliar with the *usus antiquior*, it may be useful to note the following features of this rite:

1. Before the Introit (or 'Entrance Antiphon') come the prayers at the foot of the altar. It is as this point that the *Confiteor* occurs, quite separately from the *Kyrie*. The *Kyrie* itself is nine-fold, not six-fold.
2. Before the gospel there is generally only one reading, which is followed, not by a responsorial psalm, but

by a gradual (two verses, normally from a psalm).

3. The gospel is recited facing north (this is more striking at a Solemn Mass), and the epistle facing the altar.

4. Many of the unchanging prayers are recited by the celebrant in a low voice.

5. The 'Our Father' is recited by the celebrant alone, except for the last clause, which is recited by the server (at low Mass) or by all present (at Sung or Solemn Mass).

6. The final blessing is given after the dismissal, not before.

7. In general, when the celebrant is addressing God, he faces east (either true east or 'liturgical east').

Finally, Scriptural quotations are drawn from the Douay-Rheims bible, as translating the Vulgate text used by most of the authors; except that in rendering Canticles 5:14 I have combined the Douay with the Revised Standard Version, for greater clarity.

Thomas Crean O.P.
Blackfriars
Cambridge

I am not competent to sing all, much less to know accurately, and to reveal their mysteries to others.

(Dionysius, Ecclesiastical Hierarchy, III, XI)

PART I

THE SACRIFICE
AND THE SETTING

THE SACRIFICE

St Vincent Ferrer: From the beginning of the world, God has willed that all men should offer sacrifice. Since he is himself the source whence all things come to us, he wills that we should make some offering to him.

Council of Trent: On the night he was betrayed, our Lord left to the Church, his beloved spouse, a visible sacrifice, such as the nature of man requires.

St Alphonsus: The sacrifice of the Mass has been instituted for four ends: to honour God; to satisfy for our sins; to thank God for his benefits; to obtain divine graces. It is the same sacrifice as that once offered on Calvary, with this difference, that on Calvary the blood of Jesus Christ was really shed, but on the altar it is shed only in a mystical, unbloody manner.

St John Fisher: For his body, under the appearance of bread, sets forth to us the body that hung exsanguine upon the Cross; and his blood, under the appearance of wine, recalls the blood as poured out for us upon the Cross; and so this mystery is the monument and memorial of Christ as he suffered for us.

St Bonaventure: Therefore, whatever is done in the Mass, and all its ornaments and ceremonies, symbolise nothing other than this passion of Christ.

St Lawrence of Brindisi: The heretics call the sacrifice histrionic and theatrical, as if it consisted only in the apparel of sacred vestments and ceremonies. Yet the essence of the sacrifice is not in ceremonies, nor in prayers, not in readings from sacred Scripture: these are used for their beauty, and to stir up devotion.

St Gregory the Great: This sacrifice alone has the power of saving the soul from eternal death, for it presents to us mystically the death of the only-begotten Son. Though he is now risen from the dead and dies no more, and *death has no more power over him*, yet living in himself immortal and incorruptible he is again immolated for us in the mystery of the holy Sacrifice.

St Paschasius: Since we fall each day, Christ is mystically offered for us each day, and his passion is passed down in a mystery. And as by dying once he overcame death, so daily he forgives the sins that return, through this sacrament of his body and blood.

St Leonard: For myself, I believe that were it not for holy Mass, the world would at this moment be in the abyss, unable to bear up under the load of its iniquities.

St Cyprian: The passion of our Lord is the sacrifice that we offer.

THE CHURCH

St Thomas Aquinas: The building in which this sacrament is celebrated symbolizes the Church and is called a church. It is consecrated to show that the Church has been made holy by the passion of Christ, and to show the holiness required of those who are to receive this sacrament.

St John Chrysostom: For a church is not a barber's shop or a chemist's or a market stall: it is the dwelling of angels and of archangels; it is the kingdom of God; it is heaven itself. If someone gave you entrance into heaven, you would not dare to speak a word, not even if you should see your own brother or father. Likewise in the church, only spiritual things may be spoken, for this is heaven.

Ven. Louis of Granada: Twice on entering Jerusalem, Christ went directly to the temple and when he found persons buying and selling there, he made a scourge out of ropes and drove them from the temple, spilling their money over the floor and upsetting their tables, saying, *My house is a house of prayer, but you have made it a den of thieves.* Thus Christ shows us how the Church of God is profaned and what an insult it is to God to use his temple for anything other than that for which it was built: to pray, to offer sacrifice, to preach.

St Thomas Aquinas: Some say, and not without plausibility, that simply by entering a consecrated church a man may obtain remission of venial sins, just as he may by being sprinkled with blessed water. In support of this, they quote the psalm which says, *Lord, thou hast blessed thy land; thou has forgiven the iniquity of thy people.*

Ven. Louis of Granada: On entering the church, a man must leave behind any authority he has over other men, for before God no man has any authority. Again, the cares and anxieties which a man has in regard to his home, family and business or work are good, but they should be left at the door of the church, except when he wants to speak to God about them.

St Vincent Ferrer: Therefore holy water is used on entering a church. A man makes the sign of the Cross on his forehead to seal up his mind and heart and mouth, lest he should think or speak of any worldly thing.

Paul VI: Not only while the sacrifice is offered and the sacrament is received, but as long as the Eucharist is kept in our churches and oratories, Christ is truly the Emmanuel, that is, 'God with us'. Day and night he is in our midst, he dwells with us, full of grace and truth. He restores morality, nourishes virtues, consoles the afflicted, strengthens the weak.

St John Chrysostom: Do you not know that God has placed churches in the cities as ports in the sea, that those who come thither for shelter from the storms of this world may find perfect peace?

THE EAST

St Robert Bellarmine: Two things are noteworthy about the churches that remain from ancient times. One is that they almost all possess three parts, in the likeness of Solomon's temple. They have a vestibule before the entrance, a nave, and the sanctuary, where none go but the priests and the clergy who minister there. The second is that they are normally directed to the east.

St Gregory of Nyssa: We turn ourselves to the east to pray. Not that God may only be seen there, for he is everywhere, and is not limited to any particular place; but because our first home was in the east. I mean that dwelling that we had in Paradise, from which we were expelled – for *God planted a paradise in Eden in the east*.

St Augustine: We turn to the east when we stand to pray, since this is where the sun and the stars rise. It is not, of course, as if God were there alone and had forsaken the rest of creation. Rather, when these earthly bodies of ours are turned towards the more excellent, heavenly bodies, our minds are thereby prompted to turn towards the most excellent being, that is, to our Lord.

Strabo: Yet at Rome, in the church which the ancients

called the Pantheon, and in the church of St Peter, prince of the apostles, there are altars facing not only towards the east, but also in other directions. When such arrangements are made by due authority or from necessity, I should not dare to find fault with them. Yet the more common and reasonable custom is that we should pray towards the east.

St Thomas Aquinas: It is also fitting to do this because of Christ, who is *the light of the world*, and is called *the Orient*.

St Robert Bellarmine: When our Lord died on the Cross, he was looking towards the west. So we pray facing east, as if to look at the face of the Crucified. And since he *ascends above the heaven of heavens to the east*, we, so to speak, accompany him as he ascends by our prayers and petitions. And finally, it is believed that he will come from the east in judgement: *For as lightning cometh out of the east, and appeareth even into the west, so shall also the coming of the Son of man be.*

THE TIME

St Clement of Rome: It was Christ's command that the offering of gifts and the conduct of public services should not be haphazard or irregular, but should take place at fixed times and hours.

St Cyprian: It behoved Christ to offer about the evening of the day, that the very hour of sacrifice might show the setting and the evening of the world; as it is written, *all the people of the synagogue of the children of Israel shall kill it in the evening.* And again, *Let the lifting up of my hands be an evening sacrifice.* But we celebrate the resurrection of our Lord in the morning.

St Thomas Aquinas: Normally, Mass must be celebrated in the day, and not at night, because Christ himself is present in the sacrament, who said, *I must work the works of him that sent me, whilst it is day: the night cometh, when no man can work. As long as I am in the world, I am the light of the world.* Again, in celebrating this mystery, we represent our Lord's passion: and since his passion was performed from the third hour to the ninth hour, this sacrament is normally performed in the Church in a solemn way during this period of the day. It is celebrated at the third hour on feast days, for this is when Christ was crucified by the tongues of the Judaeans.

Dom Guéranger: Also, this was the hour at which the Holy Ghost came down upon the Church; and the Church invokes this divine Spirit who by his very presence gives warmth to her love and prepares her to offer the great sacrifice.

St Thomas Aquinas: It is celebrated at noon on lesser days, for this is when he was crucified by the hands of the soldiers. On fast days it is celebrated at the ninth hour, when *crying with a loud voice he gave up the ghost.* Yet Mass may be celebrated earlier in the morning, if need be.

St Robert Bellarmine: The ancients offered the holy mysteries between the third hour and the ninth, because on fasting days the fast was not broken until the ninth hour. But ordinarily now the mysteries are celebrated between the first hour, that is, dawn, and midday.

Amalarius: There are those so imbued with divine love that they do not wish the day to pass without offering the sacrifice to God, and out of necessity must offer it later than the ninth hour. I do not think that these should be thought to act rashly and contrary to the apostolic norms, for they have a weighty motive. In the same way, our Lord defended the disciples who had been reproved for plucking the ears of corn on the Sabbath, by the example of David, who when urged by hunger, ate the consecrated loaves.

THE FAST

St Augustine: It is clear that when the disciples first received the Body, they did not receive it fasting. Would it therefore be right to blame the whole Church for this, that it is always received fasting? No: for it has pleased the Holy Spirit that in honour of so great a sacrament, no other food should enter the mouth of a Christian before the body of our Lord. This custom is observed throughout the whole world. Our Saviour himself gave no precept about this; he left it to the apostles to arrange.

St Robert Bellarmine: Luther mocks the witness of this great doctor, saying, 'Should it be forbidden priests to breathe or to live before Mass, in case some vapour or air should enter the mouth of a Christian before the body of the Lord?' But this is a horrible, and indeed diabolical impudence, not only to insult the whole Church without reason but also to twist the words of Augustine. For Augustine does not say that nothing should enter the mouth of a Christian before our Lord's body, but that no other food should enter first.

St Thomas Aquinas: This fast also shows that Christ and his charity should have first place in our hearts, according to the words, *Seek ye first the kingdom of God.*

St Paschasius: Most rightly do we receive holy communion fasting. For when self-control reigns in the body and fleshly desires are restrained, the mind gains a new strength for understanding and discerning. So our inner man is first satisfied by this food, and our noblest part is fed with heavenly delights.

St Antoninus: For a man finds it easier to practise devotion when he is fasting, than when he has dined.

St Robert Bellarmine: Luther objects with those words of the Apostle, *If any man be hungry, let him eat at home*, where the apostle seems to allow someone who cannot or will not fast to take food at home and then to go to church to receive communion. But this text has two possible meanings. First, the sense may be, 'If someone cannot remain fasting in the church for so long a time, let him eat first at home and then come to church.' That is how Anselm understands it, though he adds that the one who has taken food and come to church must not receive the Eucharist. Or else the meaning is, 'If someone is in the church and cannot bear his hunger, let him go home and eat there, not in the church.' Not that the apostle desires that this should be done; rather, he is shaming those men addicted to gluttony, indicating that they are unworthy of Holy Communion, and should be sent away from the church. And this seems the truer interpretation.

St Antoninus: While it is sometimes permitted to receive communion when one is not fasting, for example, if a sick man cannot delay because of the danger of death, it is never permitted to celebrate if one is not fasting, not even on account of the precept of a lawful superior, unless it come from the pope, who alone can dispense in this matter.

St John Chrysostom: For just as the crown comes at the end of the Olympic games, so at the end of the fast comes a pure communion.

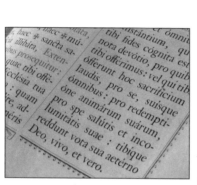

THE LANGUAGE

St Thomas Aquinas: One may note that in the liturgy of the Mass, which represents the Passion, some things are said in Greek, such as *Kyrie, eleison*, some in Hebrew, such as *Alleluia, Sabaoth* and *Amen*; and some in Latin, as is obvious. This is done because the inscription on Christ's cross was written in these three languages.

St Robert Bellarmine: The language in which the sacraments are administered is not a matter of divine law. Yet for many serious reasons it has seemed to the Church, and to the Holy Spirit who rules her, that they should not be administered in the vernacular, unless perhaps by necessity. For the majesty of divine worship surely requires a language that is more weighty and venerable than those which are in common use, if this is possible. Just as in administering the sacraments we use another building, other vestments and other vessels than those in common, daily use, so in just the same way, it seems, we should use another tongue. We do not say that Latin is holier or even weightier than other languages, if we consider the bare words, but rather that the very fact of its being not in common use makes it weightier and more venerable.

Blessed John XXIII: The Catholic Church has a dignity far surpassing that of every merely human society, since it was founded by Christ the Lord. It is altogether fitting, therefore, that the language she uses should be noble, majestic and non-vernacular. In addition, the Latin language is a most effective bond, joining together the present age of the Church with ages past and yet to come. It is a maternal voice, acceptable to countless nations.

Paul VI: Should that language of great spiritual power which transcends the boundaries of the nations be removed from our choirs, and that melody be removed which proceeds from the inmost sanctuary of the soul, where faith dwells and charity burns – that is, Gregorian chant – then would our choirs be like to an extinguished candle, which no longer gives light, or attracts the eyes and minds of men.

St Vincent Ferrer: Perhaps someone will say, 'I do not know Latin': then think of God, or think of the prayer that you are offering.

St Thomas Aquinas: Three kinds of attention are possible when we offer vocal prayers. First, we may attend to the words, lest we make a mistake in what we say. Next, we may attend to the meaning of the words. Finally, we may attend to the goal of our prayer, namely to God and to the thing for which we pray. This last is the most important kind of attention, and can be enjoyed even by the uneducated. And sometimes the mind is borne so powerfully to God by this form of attention that it is no longer aware of anything else.

TRADITION

St Robert Bellarmine: Traditions are divine, apostolic or ecclesiastical. Divine traditions are those which Christ taught the apostles, but which are not written in holy Scripture. Apostolic traditions are those which the apostles instituted, though not without the guidance of the Holy Spirit, but did not write down, such as the Lenten fast. Ecclesiastical traditions are those ancient customs that were begun by the prelates of the Church, or by the people, and which have gradually obtained the force of law, by the tacit consent of all.

St Isidore: What is done in the liturgy is laid down partly by the authority of Scripture, partly by apostolic tradition and the customs of the universal Church.

St Innocent I: Who could be ignorant or unaware that what was passed on to the Roman Church by Peter, Prince of the Apostles, and has been guarded until now must be preserved by all? For it is evident that in all Italy, in Gaul, in Spain, in Africa and Sicily and in the islands nearby, none of the churches has instituted anything but what the venerable apostle Peter and the priests who succeeded him have established.

Strabo: Nor should we be surprised to learn that the rites have gradually developed, for there was room for many important things to be introduced. Even today, when we have such abundance, we see that some new readings and collects and others forms of praise are still being added. For here too must the prophetic word be fulfilled, *Many shall pass over, and knowledge shall be manifold.*

St Anselm: If there were only one manner of celebration throughout the whole Church, that would be good and worthy of praise. Yet in fact there are many variant customs, which however involve no disagreement about the substance of the sacrament, or about its power, or about the faith. Since these customs cannot all be harmonised, I judge that they should rather be allowed to exist together in peace than that some should be condemned, which would cause conflict and scandal. For we have learned from the holy fathers that, provided the unity of charity be maintained in Catholic faith, variety of customs is not harmful.

St Augustine: The practices of God's people and the ordinances of the fathers must be regarded as laws. And just as those who defy the divine laws are made to obey them, so also must those be who despise the customs of the Church.

St John Cassian: Even when the reason for it has not been grasped, it certainly behoves us to yield to the authority of the fathers, and to a custom of our forebears which has existed for so many years up until our own day, and to maintain it, as it was passed on of old.

St Thomas Aquinas: Indeed the very change of a law is injurious to the health of a society, since it is above all custom that upholds the rule of law. So no human law must be changed unless the harm wrought by the change will in some way be compensated, as when the new law brings some very great and obvious benefit, or when it is a case of necessity, or when the established custom was manifestly unjust or extremely harmful.

Ven. John Henry Newman: We must be aware of the great error of making changes on no more definite basis than their abstract fitness, alleged scripturalness, or adoption by the ancients. Such changes are rightly called innovations; those which spring from existing institutions, opinions, and feelings are called developments, and may be recommended, without invidiousness, as improvements.

St John Chrysostom: It is tradition: seek no further.

PART II

THE RITE

Before the Beginning

St Gregory the Great: We must offer unto God the daily sacrifice of tears and the daily sacrifice of his body and blood. For what right believing Christian can doubt that in the very hour of the sacrifice, at the words of the priest, the heavens be opened, and the choirs of angels be present in that very mystery of Jesus Christ? But necessary it is that when we do these things, we should also by contrition of heart sacrifice ourselves unto almighty God. For when we celebrate the mystery of our Lord's passion, we ought to imitate what we then do: for then shall it truly be a sacrifice for us unto God, if we offer ourselves also to him in sacrifice.

Durandus: The priest comes forth from the holy chamber, clad in sacred vestments, and approaches the altar, to show that Christ, the hope of the nations, came forth from his secret dwelling in the heavens, clothed in holy flesh drawn from the spotless Virgin, and entered into this world.

St Thomas Aquinas: Just as the celebration of this sacrament is the image of Christ's passion, so the altar represents the cross on which he was immolated in his visible appearance.

St Alphonsus: He says, 'In the name of the Father and

of the Son and of the Holy Spirit', thus declaring that he offers the sacrifice by the authority of the three Persons of the Blessed Trinity.

St Robert Bellarmine: Before the beginning of the Mass, the psalm *Judge me, O God, and distinguish my cause from the nation that is not just* is recited, and a general confession is made.

Dom Guéranger: This psalm was selected on account of the verse *Introibo ad altare Dei:* I will go unto the altar of God.

St Augustine: There is an invisible and heavenly altar, which the unjust can never approach. No one comes to that heavenly altar, but he who comes to this altar with care. He will find his life there, if at this altar, he *distinguishes his cause.*

Durandus: Before the priest or bishop ascends the steps of the altar and performs his sacred office, he takes thought for himself and bows low before the altar, to symbolise how Christ emptied himself, when he bowed the heavens and came down, taking the form of a servant. And considering how Solomon said, *The just man in the beginning is the accuser of himself*, he makes confession to those about him.

St Robert Bellarmine: Now, no one can object to the psalm, nor to the confession insofar as it is made to God and to those present with us. Yet our opponents do object to the confession insofar as it is made to the saints. For they say that the saints cannot hear it, being so far off. But the Catholic Church makes no doubt that just as the saints know our prayers, so also they hear our confessions. For the practice of invoking the saints has always been found among true Christians, and the miracles that have been worked in all ages through the invocation of the saints prove that they hear our prayers. Therefore, we confess to God, to the saints, and to the Church on earth, for we offend against them all by our sins, just as one said in the Gospel of St Luke, *I have sinned against heaven and before thee.*

Dom Guéranger: The confession has this prerogative, in common with all the other sacramentals that its recitation produces the forgiveness of venial sins, provided we be contrite for them.

St Albert: The one who is to sing the Mass kisses the altar on first approaching it. He does this so that he may speak words of true peace to the people. *And coming, he preached peace to you that were far off, and peace to them that were nigh.*

Blessed Hyacinth Cormier: It is a kiss of gladness, that he should have been granted the honour and happiness of celebrating the Mass.

Durandus: The priest kisses the sacred altar to show that when Christ came to us, he joined holy Church to himself: as it is said in the bridal song, *Let him kiss me with the kiss of his mouth.* And he places his hands upon the altar to show that charity, which is denoted by the kiss, must be supported by good works.

St John Chrysostom: Awesome is the altar on which the divine victim is immolated! From paradise there went forth a spring whose visible waters spread out on every side. From this Table, it is a spring of spiritual waters that gushes forth.

INTROIT

St Thomas Aquinas: This sacrament embraces the entire mystery of our salvation, and so it is celebrated with greater solemnity than the other sacraments. And because it is written, *Keep thy foot, when thou goest into the house of God*, and *Before prayer prepare thy soul*, before this mystery is celebrated, preparation is made so that what follows may be worthily accomplished. The first part of this preparation is divine praise, which is accomplished by the Introit. As the psalm says, *The sacrifice of praise shall glorify me: and there is the way by which I will shew him the salvation of God.*

St Robert Bellarmine: The Introit is composed of an antiphon, the psalm, and the *Gloria Patri*. Most authors agree that Pope Celestine[9] introduced it: yet this statement must be qualified. For he ordained that the 150 psalms of David should be sung before the sacrifice; but later, to avoid prolixity, certain verses were selected that seemed more suited to arouse devotion, and the singing of entire psalms was left to the divine office. Nor was Celestine the very first to attach psalms to the sacrifice, though he was perhaps the first who ordained this to be done at Rome.

---

9. St Celestine I, who died in the year 432 AD.

St Alphonsus: It is usually in the Introit that the Church proposes the subject of the feast that is celebrated. Mention is made therein of some divine mystery, or of the Blessed Virgin, or of some other saint whom the Church honours on that day.

Amalarius: All that is done in the liturgy of the Mass up to the reading of the gospel concerns the first coming of our Lord, and his life until the moment when he made haste to Jerusalem for his passion. The Introit recalls the company of prophets who preceded him.

St Germanus: It is sung in the likeness of those ancient fathers who lived before the Deluge, and thundered forth in mystic words the coming of the Christ. Such was Enoch, the seventh from Adam, who prophesied, saying, *Behold the Lord cometh with thousands of his saints to execute judgement upon all.*

St Antoninus: The holy fathers and prophets who lived before Christ longed for his coming, and sent before them their desires, works and praises. For this reason, the Introit is said at the start of the Mass, to denote their desires. It is followed by the verse, which represents their works. But since after our works, glory must be given to God the Trinity, after the Introit comes the *Gloria Patri*.

St Albert: *My soul hath desired thee in the night: yea, and with my spirit within me in the morning early I will watch to thee.* Isaias speaks these words out of the desire that the ancient fathers had, as they sighed after the presence of Christ in the flesh. The whole time that passed from the dark sin of our first parents until the light that rose in the darkness for the upright of heart – as it is written,

Unto you that fear my name, the Sun of justice shall arise, and health in his wings – this whole time, I say, is called one of deep darkness, since the light of evangelical truth was not yet shining save in the shadowy figures of the Law, and the light of grace and goodness was beclouded by the gloomy power of sin, so that all sat in darkness and in the shadow of the first death. It was in this night, therefore, that Isaias declared, *My soul hath desired thee in the night.* Nor is this strange: for the light that sometimes gleams in the good words and deeds of the saints could not disperse that darkness, nor could its cold be warmed by their charity. So it is said, *No power of fire could give them light, neither could the bright flames of the stars enlighten that horrible night,* for even the brief sparkling of the saints was swallowed up after death by the darkness of the limbo beneath. And so the soul of Isaias and the souls of the other saints were sighing after Christ, the true light, who puts darkness to flight. Breathed upon by the Holy Ghost, the Church expresses this cry of the ancient fathers, yearning also for the coming of Christ. In that chant of the Mass which is called the Introit, she lifts up her voice, suddenly overcome by a feeling of desire. So begins the Mass, which is the coming of Christ in the sacrament. Crying out, then, with this love, the Church in her Introit seeks the coming of our Lord, remembering the desire of the fathers who longed for the coming of Christ in the flesh.

St Thomas Aquinas: Even if some do not understand what things are being sung, yet they know why they are sung, namely, to give praise to God; and this is enough to stir up their devotion.

St Augustine: I shall never have too much of the wonderful joy that comes to me when I think of the depth of God's plan for man's salvation. I have listened eagerly to the melodies of the Church and her sweet song, to the canticles and the hymns. Yes, those sounds flowed into my ears and the pure stream of truth ran through my heart and tears flowed forth from my eyes, and it was good for me to be there.

St Albert: There was sometimes in the ancient churches the custom that an entire psalm would be sung, with the antiphon repeated at every verse. This is no longer done, to avoid prolixity; but it is repeated once, so that the Church may recall and express the oft-repeated cry of the ancient fathers. Now some one may object that not all Introits express in words the desire of the ancient fathers, but only those Introits that are used in Advent. They might say that on the feasts of the saints, no mention is made of the ancient desire for Christ's coming. We reply that the fathers did not wait for Christ as if he were simply a private person; they waited for him as the Christ promised to all men, who carried with him an infinitude of graces, who would come as a king surrounded by the throng of all the saints, and in whose royal courts all the saints would dwell. Thus Jude, in his epistle, declares that Enoch, the seventh from Adam, prophesied and said, *Behold the Lord cometh with thousands of his saints, to execute judgement upon all, and to reprove the ungodly for all the works of their ungodliness, whereby they have done ungodly.* This was how the ancient fathers longed for him; they desired him to come in his kingly beauty and in the beauty of his royal court.

KYRIE, ELEISON

St Thomas Aquinas: After the Introit, our preparation continues as we recall the wretchedness of our present state and ask for God's mercy. To the Father we say three times, *Kyrie eleison*, to the Son we say three times, *Christe eleison*, and to the Holy Spirit we say three times, *Kyrie eleison*. Each invocation is repeated three times to denote the three elements that make up our wretchedness: ignorance, sin, and the suffering due to sin. Or else, each invocation is said thrice to show that all the divine persons dwell mutually in each other.

St Robert Bellarmine: It is a most ancient custom among the Latins to sing this litany in Greek. For when St Gregory was accused of having introduced the *Kyrie eleison* and other Greek customs into the Latin Church, he replied that he was conserving or restoring the ancient customs of the Roman Church.

St Gregory: Among the Greeks all say the *Kyrie, Eleison* together; but with us it is said by the clerks, and responded to by the people. Also, as often as it is said, *Christe Eleison* is said also, which is not said at all among the Greeks.

St Albert: If the clergy express the desire of the ancient fathers in the Introit, the *Kyrie, eleison* represents the

42

faithful seconding this plea. This is why it was put into the Mass: it represents the spontaneous obedience by which the people are at one with their clergy.

Amalarius: Or, the *Kyrie eleison* recalls those prophets who lived at the time of the coming of our Lord, among whom were Zachary, and John his son.

St Albert: By sin, we fall into a three-fold wretchedness We fall, first, into that subjection which is slavery to sin. Secondly, we fall into poverty, for sin despoils us of the goods of grace. Thirdly, we are trampled upon by worthless demons on whom we ought rather to have trampled, since they are slaves. No wonder, then, that when the faithful people hear the clergy call upon our Lord to come, with the same desire that the fathers had of old, they too, perceiving this threefold misery of theirs, cry out together with their clergy, *Kyrie, eleison*, that his mercy may raise those who call to him from their threefold misery. And once we have called upon our Lord in this way, we next call upon him as our mediator, the one who saves our nature and makes it holy. Three times the cry resounds, *Christe, eleison*. 'Christ' means the Anointed, and oil is used for anointing, for light and for nourishment. Therefore the people, feeling their sickness, suffering from darkness, loathing their unsavouriness, cry out thrice to the anointed one.

St Vincent Ferrer: We can put forward three reasons why Christ should hear us and have mercy on us: because he is our brother; because he is our Redeemer; because he is our God. Therefore in the Mass we say three times, *Christe, eleison*.

St Albert: Then *Kyrie, eleison* is again sung thrice. Now 'Lord' is a name of power, and power does three things. It avenges iniquity by just judgement. It restrains the evil will by its severity. It defends virtue and goodness by equitable laws. Therefore the faithful, who feel themselves to be guilty of iniquity, cry out a first time, *Kyrie, eleison*, calling upon the mercy of our Lord, that they may not know the avenging sword. A second time the faithful cry out, *Kyrie, eleison*, for they know their wills to be rebellious, and they desire him to check their rebellion, yet in mercy, not in wrath and fury. Still a third time they cry out. For they feel that those things within them that agree to the law of God are not yet free, and so they say, *Kyrie, eleison*, that they may be made free.

Durandus: This invocation is made nine times, so that the order of human beings may be restored and take its place with the nine orders of angels.

St Albert: It is asked, 'Why is this invocation made in Greek and not in Latin?' One of the reasons given by the Fathers is that the highest natural wisdom flourished in Greece. And to show that to call on God's mercy is the highest wisdom, this invocation is sung in Greek. Again, the faith came to us Latins from the Greeks; Peter and Paul came to the Latins from the Greeks and from them came salvation for us. And so that we may be mindful that this grace came to us from the Greeks, we preserve even now the very words and syllables with which the divine mercy was first invoked by the people. For we owe this reverence to the fathers, that the traditions which they instituted should be followed also by us.

St Alphonsus: Thereby is shown the union that exists between the Greek and Latin Church.

St Thomas Aquinas: One may note that in the liturgy of the Mass, which represents the Passion, some things are said in Greek, such as *Kyrie, eleison*, some in Hebrew, such as *Alleluia*, *Sabaoth* and *Amen*; and some in Latin, as is obvious. This is done because the inscription on Christ's cross was written in these three tongues.

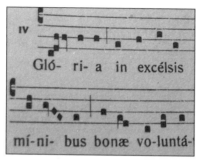

GLORIA IN EXCELSIS

*Glory to God
in the highest, and on earth peace to men of good will.
We praise thee. We bless thee. We adore thee.
We glorify thee. We give thee thanks for thy great
glory: O Lord God, heavenly king,
God the Father almighty.
O Lord Jesus Christ, the only-begotten Son:
O Lord God, Lamb of God, Son of the Father:
who takest away the sins of the world,
have mercy upon us.
Who takest away the sins of the world,
receive our prayer.
Who sittest at the right hand of the Father,
have mercy on us.
For thou only art holy. Thou only art Lord.
Thou only, O Jesus Christ, are most high, together
with the Holy Ghost,
in the glory of God the Father. Amen.*

St Thomas Aquinas: The third part of the preparation consists in recalling the heavenly glory to which we are tending after the present life and our wretchedness. So on feast days, *Gloria in excelsis* is sung, to recall that heavenly glory.

St Albert: Now the *Gloria* is not sung on ferial days. Nor is it sung on days when the Church fasts, unless it be a joyful fast as in Whitsuntide. For on these days we seek to make satisfaction for sins committed, fearful of divine wrath, and we call to mind the peace that has not yet been granted to us.

St Robert Bellarmine: Almost all agree that Pope St Telesphorus[10] first laid down that this be sung at Mass.

Strabo: He ordained that it be said before the sacrifice, so that the minds of those present might be calmed by the beauty of this angelic song in preparation for such great holiness.

St Albert: God's mercy has never been lacking to those who call upon him. Nor is his mercy lacking today; nor shall it ever be lacking. Therefore on those days when consolation is to be offered to the people, the one who stands in the place of the Angel of great counsel, that is the bishop or priest, sings from the altar as if from the very presence of God, *Gloria in excelsis Deo*. It is as if he were saying, 'I will certainly answer your cries and I will send to you in the Sacrament the one whom I sent into the world to your fathers, that you may partake of him, and be drawn out from your evils and be filled with every good.'

Amalarius: The *Gloria in excelsis* recalls the company of angels who announced to the shepherds the joy of our Lord's birth.

---

10. Martyred in the year 136 AD.

St Albert: When the Saviour was first presented in the world, one angel sang *Gloria in excelsis Deo*; then a great multitude of the heavenly hosts praised God. Likewise, in the Mass, the bishop or priest begins. Then in memory of what is described in the gospel, the choir sings the rest of the *Gloria* to a solemn and sonorous melody.

Durandus: The one who begins takes his stand at the middle of the altar, to show that the Messiah was born when *all things were in the midst of silence*.

St Albert: The glory which is in the highest may not be attributed except to God, for he alone possesses it. Thus in the Book of Genesis, Joseph says to Pharaoh's wife, *Behold, my master hath delivered all things to me, and knoweth not what he hath in his own house: neither is there anything which is not in my power, or that he hath not delivered to me, but thee, who art his wife.* Good Joseph knew, as the apostle would later say, that *the woman is the glory of the man*. And so although he had received his lord's goods, he did not seek to possess his lord's glory.

St Thomas Aquinas: For this reason, a woman veils her head when praying. For God's glory should be revealed, but man's glory should be hidden, according to the psalm, *Not to us, O Lord, not to us; but to thy name give glory.*

St Albert: The three persons are in one and the same glory, the brightness of the eternal shining. Yet it is called *the glory of God the Father*, since the Father is the principle of the whole godhead.

St Alphonsus: God is *thanked for his glory*, because God has used our salvation for his glory by saving us through Jesus Christ.

St Albert: He is *Lord God*, and therefore powerful to save us. He is *Lamb of God*, and therefore gentle enough to suffer for us; he is *Son of the Father*, who from obedience to the Father paid Adam's debt.

St Alphonsus: Addressing herself to Jesus Christ, the Church asks him by the merits of his sacrifice to have pity on us. For our Saviour, who sacrifices himself as a victim, is at the same time God, equal to him to whom the sacrifice is offered.

Blessed Hyacinth Cormier: We should not seek in the *Gloria* a logical progression of ideas. It is, rather, an impulsive succession of acclamations and words of praise, that spring forth unplanned from the soul. Faith, the freedom of prayer, and a love that knows how to weave all things together: these are the only rules.

St Albert: The *Gloria* concludes with the word *Amen*. Sometimes this means, 'let it be done'. Sometimes it means truly, as when our Lord says, *Amen, amen, I say to you*. Sometimes it means 'a true thing', or truth. Thus in the Apocalypse, our Lord says, *These things saith the Amen, the faithful and true witness*. And this is what it means here, as if the people are saying, '*Amen*: what you have sung is true.'

DOMINUS VOBISCUM

St Albert: *To the festivals he added beauty, and set in order the solemn times even to the end of his life.* These words may be applied to Blessed Gregory.[11] He pruned from the rites what was superfluous, and ensured that all the necessary elements were well-ordered. So having set in order the first part of the Mass, where our Lord is invoked by the desire of the clergy and the acclamation of the people, and speaks to them good and peaceful words, promising his people peace by his own coming, Blessed Gregory also set in order the second part. This consists in words of instruction about the one who is to come, and it continues until the Offertory exclusively. First comes instruction for the imperfect, and then instruction for the perfect, about perfection. The instruction of the imperfect has three parts: a preparation, the instruction itself, and what follows from it. The preparation is the *Dominus vobiscum* and the collect.

St Peter Damian: This form of greeting was not instituted recently by the powers of human thought.

---

11. Pope Gregory the Great.

Rather, it comes from the ancient authority of the sacred word. In the book of Ruth, when Booz greeted the reapers, he said to them, *Dominus vobiscum*.

Amalarius: And no one should doubt but that Christ himself made that greeting through Booz, in whose loins he was.

Durandus: For Booz became a type of Christ, by taking Ruth the foreign woman, the Moabitess, to be his wife.

St Albert: The one who is in the place of God turns his face to the people, to show that God's countenance is reflected in the writings of the law and the prophets, as in a mirror, and is shown forth clearly in the reading of the apostles. *The Lord turn his countenance to thee, and give thee peace.* A bishop and a priest use different greetings because the bishop exercises a higher office, in the place of Christ, and so he uses the very words of Christ when speaking to his subjects. For the first greeting that Christ made to the apostles after the resurrection was *Peace be to you*. But the priest holds a lower rank, and so does not dare to use the same words.

St Thomas Aquinas: At a solemn celebration of the Mass, there must be a multitude present. But at private Masses, it is sufficient to have one server. This server takes the place of the whole Catholic people, and so the priest greets him in the plural.

St Peter Damian: For the Church of Christ is bound together by so great a bond of charity as to be one in many and yet, by a mystery, wholly present in each. Thus the universal church may be rightly considered the one spouse of Christ; and each soul, by the mystery of the sacrament, is believed to be the Church in her integrity.

St Albert: We should consider why the people answer the priest in a different manner from that in which they were greeted. For they do not say 'may the Lord be with you', or something similar, but 'and with thy spirit'. There are three reasons for this. The first is that the priest, when he stands at the altar, must be entirely in the spirit. The second is that the spirit of man frequently goes astray. The third is that what happens at the altar is clearly a work done by spiritual power. So the one who stands at the altar must be nothing but spirit, and must think nothing of the body or of the cares of the world.

St Peter Damian: The people say 'and with thy spirit'. That is, may the omnipotent God be with your soul, so that you may pray to him worthily for our salvation.

St Germanus: The priest becomes more worthy to bless the people when by God's will he receives these blessings from the mouth of the whole people.

St Albert: There is a figure of this in the book of Genesis. When Abraham was about to go off to sacrifice his son, *he said to his young men, 'Stay you here with the ass: I and the boy will go with speed as far as yonder, and after we have worshipped, will return to you.'* The servants are anxieties and worries about the necessities of this life. The ass, an animal that cannot be disciplined and yet is useful for bearing burdens, is our body: for this is lazy and will not accept discipline, yet bears the burden of labour. The boy is a pure spirit, and the patriarch prefigures the priest. And so the priest who is about to sacrifice the Son of God must leave behind his anxieties and cares and the weight of the body, and advance to the altar for the sacrifice with his spirit alone. Hence the people say, *et cum spiritu tuo*. And just as the greeting *Dominus vobiscum* is taken from what Booz says to the reapers, so the reply is taken from the second letter to St Timothy: *The Lord Jesus Christ be with thy spirit.*

COLLECT

St Thomas Aquinas: The fourth part of the preparation is the prayer that the priest makes for the people, asking that they may be reckoned worthy of these great mysteries.

St Albert: The prayer is called the 'Collect', either because the priest, who knows the secrets of the people, collects these secrets and offers them to our Lord, or because it is made for the people, who are collected in the communion of our Lord. For the work of God is always to collect, as the work of the devil is to disperse.

St Robert Bellarmine: The ancients called the Mass itself 'the collect', since this was the object for which the people came together. In ancient days, also, Christians never met together, without finishing with a prayer.

St Alphonsus: In this prayer are asked of God the graces bound up with the mystery of the day, for example at Easter, the grace to rise with Christ, and at the Ascension the grace to dwell with him in spirit in heaven; or we ask for the graces that we wish to receive through the intercession of the saint whose feast we are celebrating.

Amalarius: The collect recalls what our Lord did when he was about twelve, when he went up to Jerusalem and sat in the temple in the midst of the doctors, listening to them and asking them questions.[12]

Gloss: It may also be said that the collect represents the prayer that Christ offered to his Father during his hidden life, before his public ministry.

St Albert: The number of collects said should be uneven, either one, three, five or seven, but no more. For even numbers are based on the number two, and two is a departure from unity. This is why, according to Augustine, when God created the world, he did not bless the works of the second day, even though he blessed the works of all the other days. And so it is said that 'God loves uneven numbers',[13] because God detests division in all matters. Again, Christ, giving us the 'Our Father', taught us seven petitions that explicitly ask for all that is necessary, and that is why we should not offer more than seven collects. To do more than this would be *to speak much*, which would cause weariness and lessen devotion.

Durandus: The priest turns to the east, since Christ sought not his own will, but his Father's. Indeed, he turns his back to the people, expressing what our Lord said to Moses, *Thou shalt see my hinder parts, but my face thou canst not see.*

St Thomas Aquinas: The priest raises his hands to pray, to show that his prayer is directed to God on behalf of

---

12. The similarity lies in this, that as Christ interrupted his hidden life by a public appearance in the sanctuary of God, so the priest, at a solemn Mass, comes briefly to the altar to sing the collect.
13. Not in Scripture: in Virgil's *Eclogues.*

the people. So it is said in Lamentations, *Let us lift up our hearts with our hands to the Lord in the heavens.*

St Vincent Ferrer: We stretch out two hands in prayer. With the right we pray for spiritual blessings, and with the left for temporal ones. Our poor teach us to act like this, for this is how they beg, when they ask alms from the rich. And the rich man is Christ.

St Albert: The conclusion of almost all the collects begins *through our Lord*. For we are heard not for our own merits, but for Christ's, and so it is right to finish our prayer in the name of Christ. This is the name of the mediator, who stretches his hands towards both sides, that is, towards God and towards man. For just as we can take no fire from the sun, which is so far off, unless we use a beryl or a crystal or something of that sort; so also we cannot draw any grace from our heavenly Father, from whom we have become estranged by sin, except through a mediator who will be close both to him and to us.

St Vincent Ferrer: Many saints say that whereas antichrist will apply all of Christ's other titles to himself, he will persecute the name 'Jesus'. So Christians, on the contrary, must pay the greatest honour to the name of Jesus, bowing their heads whenever it is named in the church.

St Robert Bellarmine: There are some collects that are directed to the Son, but they are very few, and perhaps not as ancient as the others. Perhaps the Church took care to direct some collects to the Son lest anyone suppose that only the Father might be addressed in eloquent language.

St Albert: The *Amen*, may be understood to apply to the prayer as a whole, and then it means 'Let what you have asked from God be done.' Or it may be taken as referring to the conclusion, and then it means 'It is true: God the Trinity is living for all the ages of ages.'

St Augustine: Amen is a Hebrew term. Men have abstained from translating it, in order to throw a veil of reverence over so mysterious a word. Not that they wanted to lock it up, but only to prevent it from becoming despised by being exposed.

LECTIO

St Thomas Aquinas: After the preparation comes the instruction of the faithful people, since this sacrament is *the mystery of faith*. This instruction is done initially by the teaching of the prophets and the apostles.

St Robert Bellarmine: It seems that this custom was taken from the Hebrews, among whom to this day readings from the prophets are read in the synagogue every Sabbath.

St Albert: *The Lord spoke to Moses, saying, 'Make thee two trumpets of beaten silver, wherewith thou mayst call together the multitude, when the camp is to be removed.'* The two trumpets that sound before the giver of sanctity are the subdeacon and deacon. They are silver trumpets because the delightful sound this instrument produces signifies the sweet sound of God's word instructing us. They are *beaten* silver, because each must be proved strong and patient in overcoming tribulation. The multitude of the people is convoked by these two, whenever the camp of God is to advance from virtue to virtue.

St Thomas Aquinas: In this sacrament, some things are said by ministers, such as the teaching of the old and the new testaments. This signifies that doctrine was announced to the people by ministers sent by God.

St Albert: The subdeacon declares the doctrine of the imperfect. And since this doctrine was represented by the preaching of John the Baptist, at a time when Christ was still hidden, the subdeacon does not seek a blessing from the bishop or the priest. Likewise, he goes to the ambo without the light of candles, since he does not announce truths plainly. And if it be said that he does announce truths plainly when he reads from the writings of the Apostles, we may say that these words direct us to the gospel, from where they receive their light, and so they have no light of their own. Again, he goes with but one acolyte, for they were few who followed the preaching of John and of the law and the prophets.

Durandus: The face of the one who reads the epistle must be turned to the altar, because the preaching of John directed himself and others towards Christ, whom the altar represents.

Origen: Even if the words of Scripture seem obscure to us, yet in passing through our ears they confer no small benefit on the soul. For if the gentiles believe that certain chants, which those who practise the art call incantations, can exercise such force over serpents that they are put to sleep or brought forth from secret hiding places, even though they who chant do not understand their own words, how much more powerful should we believe to be the proclamation of the words and names of holy Scripture! Even if we do not understand what we speak with our mouths, yet those powers who are present to us understand it, and as if drawn by our chanting, they delight to come to us and bring us their aid.

St Albert: When he returns to the priest, he kisses his right hand, to show that he does not attribute his advance in virtue to himself, but to God. *The right hand of the Lord hath exalted me: the right hand of the Lord hath wrought strength.*

GRADUAL

St Thomas Aquinas: After the reading from the prophets or the apostles, the choir sings the gradual, which signifies progress in life; then an *Alleluia* is sung, to signify spiritual gladness, or else, on penitential days, a Tract, which signifies spiritual lament. For the people must gain all these things through the doctrine that has been read to them.

Durandus: The gradual follows after the epistle, because after the preaching of John, the apostles followed Christ, as John the Evangelist tells: *John stood, and two of his disciples, and beholding Jesus walking, he saith, Behold the Lamb of God. And the two disciples heard him speak, and they followed Jesus.*

St Albert: The word 'gradual' comes from 'grades', because those who have been instructed strive to pass through the different grades of the virtues. More literally, it is called the Gradual because it is sung on the grades, or steps, of the altar.

Dom Guéranger: Or, it was because of the steps which led to the ambo that this portion of the chant got the name of Gradual; just as the gradual psalms were those which the Jews used to sing whilst ascending the steps of the temple.

St Robert Bellarmine: These verses are sung lest the time should be wasted that must pass between the epistle and the gospel, as the deacon prepares to chant the latter.

St Albert: By singing the gradual, they profess that they are advancing *from virtue to virtue, until* in the teaching of the gospel, *they will see the God of gods in Sion.* That is why it has many difficult and severe passages, and notes of a low pitch, for it is always difficult to advance in virtue and so gain something good.

Amalarius: Yet by the beauty of this melody, even carnal hearts may be cut to the quick, and torn open as earth is torn in furrows. For though the hearers should have remained like deaf men at the reading of the epistle, by the gradual they may be reached.

ALLELUIA

St Albert: Since advance in virtue, signified by the Gradual, gives rise not only to mourning, because of its difficulty, but also to joy, because of the relish that the virtuous man has in his virtue, the Church has ordained that on feast days when the eternal joy is commemorated, the *Alleluia* should be sung after the Gradual. *Alleluia shall be sung in her streets*, that is, in Jerusalem.

Amalarius: The *Alleluia* refers to the gladness of heart that the apostles felt at the promises of Christ, or at the miracles that they saw to be done by him or in his name. Hence, what is sown in the Gradual is reaped in the *Alleluia*.

St Gregory: Our custom of saying the *Alleluia* is said to be derived from the Church of Jerusalem by the tradition of the blessed Jerome in the time of Pope Damasus of blessed memory.

St Bede: *Alleluia* is a Hebrew word, and it means 'praise our Lord'. It is most proper and beautiful that a general custom has prevailed in holy Church of all the faithful throughout the world singing this word of praise in the Hebrew language. In this way the whole Church is admonished that it ought now to consist in one faith, confession and love of Christ, and that in the future it ought to hurry to that fatherland in which there is no discord of minds and no disharmony of speech.

St Isidore: John in the Apocalypse states that through the revelation of the Holy Ghost he saw and heard the heavenly army of angels, *as the noise of many waters, and as the voice of great thunder*, crying *Alleluia*. So none should doubt but that this mystic praise joins to the angels those who offer it with true faith and devotion. Like *Amen*, *Alleluia* has never been translated from Hebrew into Latin. Not that its meaning is unknown; rather, as the learned say, these words have by their very antiquity, a greater and holier authority.

St Thomas Aquinas: The *Alleluia* intimates the joy that we feel in the hope of the eternal things. It is repeated, because both the soul and the body are to be clothed in glory.

St Antoninus: During paschal time, a second *Alleluia* is sung. This denotes the resurrection of both the Head and the members.

Durandus: The *Alleluia* does not so much express the joy of that far distant life, but points towards it. And though it is but one word, it has many notes for this joy is greater than can be expressed.

St Augustine: What is this jubilation, this exultant song? It is the melody that means our hearts are bursting with feelings words cannot express. And to whom does this jubilation most belong? Surely, to God who is unutterable. And does not unutterable mean 'what cannot be uttered'? If words will not come and you may not remain silent, what else can you do but let the melody soar?

TRACT

St Albert: On days set aside for penance, the Gradual is followed by the Tract. For so great is the weight of the iniquity that sin lays upon us, that we are scarce drawn toward goodness even by force.[14] Therefore, the spouse in the Canticle of Canticles cries in lamentation, *Draw me after thee*. And since this takes place with the help of penitential works, the Tract is sung with long drawn out notes that sound mournful and severe. And it often has several verses, since a man must be drawn to penance in many ways before sin is finally destroyed. He must desist from the act of sin, and pluck from his will the roots of sin, and blot out the remnants of a long habit of sin. By all these verses, then, we must be drawn as along a rough way.

Durandus: The Tract symbolises the tears of the saints, whether they follow the active way or the contemplative way. And this explains its name, since the saints in their sighing draw up their groans from the bottom of their hearts, although they rejoice in their hope.

---

14. 'Tract' means literally something 'drawn' or 'drawn out'.

Amalarius: The number 70 symbolizes the captivity of the people of God in Babylonia, for only after 70 years did they return to Jerusalem. This is why *Alleluia* is not sung by us in Septuagesima, nor is the angels' hymn, *Gloria in excelsis Deo*. The psalm says, *How shall we sing the song of the Lord in a strange land?*; and the *Gloria* and *Alleluia* are heavenly songs.

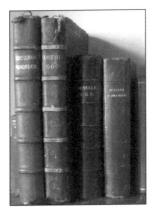

GOSPEL

St Thomas Aquinas: The people are instructed fully by the doctrine of Christ contained in the gospel. This is read by the highest of the ministers, that is, by the deacon.

Amalarius: The gospel puts us in mind of Christ's own preaching, until his entrance into Jerusalem.

Durandus: The subdeacon goes to the priest and pays reverence to him after his reading, but the deacon does this before, because the law reached its end in Christ, but the gospel took its origin from him. And he seeks a blessing, according to the word of the apostle, *How shall they preach unless they be sent?*

St Albert: The book of the gospels is taken from the altar. This is figured in the Apocalypse, where it is said, *I saw in the right hand of him that sat upon the throne, a book, written within and without, sealed with seven seals.* The altar represents God's throne, on which Christ is seated, our unseen God and king and priest. The deacon receives the book from his right hand, when he goes to evangelize in the power of God.

St Robert Bellarmine: Pope St Anastasius I[15] commanded that all who heard the gospel should stand,

---

15. He died in 401 AD.

out of reverence for our Lord speaking therein. Yet he was not the first to introduce this custom. Rather, he confirmed it, and ordered that it should also be introduced in those places where it had not previously been followed.

St Francis de Sales: When the gospel is to be read at Mass, stand up to show that you are ready and equipped to walk on the way that the gospel commands. To stir your devotion, you can say as you do so, 'Jesus Christ was made obedient unto death, even the death of the cross.'

St Albert: The deacon goes in procession preceded by two candle-bearers and a cross-bearer. The two candles signify the light of knowledge and the light of virtue, which make it possible to see what is contained in the gospel.

St Jerome: Whenever the gospel is to be read, the candles are lighted, though the dawn may be reddening the sky; not to scatter the darkness, but by way of evidencing our joy.

St Albert: The cross is borne aloft to show that the deacon who is to proclaim the gospel must glory in the cross, which gives his proclamation its power. Before them goes one holding the smoking thurible, to show that the odour of good repute, not the stench of infamy, must precede the gospel preacher.

Durandus: The smoke of incense is believed to have power to put the demon to flight. Hence, when Tobias asked the angel what use those parts of the fish were which he had been ordered to keep, the angel replied, *if thou put a little piece of its heart upon coals, the smoke thereof driveth away all kinds of devils, either from man or from woman, so that they come no more to them.*

Dom Guéranger: The epistle is merely preceded by the subdeacon's saying whence the passage comes which he is going to sing, whereas the gospel is always preceded by the words: *Dominus vobiscum.* The reason is that in the epistle, it is but the servant that speaks to us; in the gospel, it is the word of the Master himself which we are about to hear.

St Francis de Sales: Make the sign of the cross on your forehead and mouth and heart, and say, 'May God be in my heart and on my lips, that I may worthily receive his holy gospel.'

St Augustine: So far am I from blushing at the Cross of Christ, that I do not keep it in some hidden place but rather bear it on my forehead. Since the forehead is the seat of the blush of shame, he who said, *Whosoever shall be ashamed of me before men, of him will I be ashamed before my Father which is in heaven*, set, so to speak, that very ignominy which the pagans mock at, in the seat of our shame.

St Albert: The deacon stands and reads the gospel facing north. For the north is a cold and dark region: it signifies the dark and freezing malice of the devil. *From the north shall an evil break forth upon all the inhabitants of the land.* The teacher of perfection is set up in opposition to this malice, to put darkness to flight with the light of truth, and with the heat of charity to keep the north from freezing the hearts of his hearers. It is as if he were speaking those words, *Arise, O north, and come, O south: blow through my garden and let the spices thereof flow.* The north must arise, that is, be expelled, so that the warm south wind may come, and the fragrance of the virtues make itself felt.

Durandus: He turns his face to the north, to show that we must be armed by gospel doctrine and by the preaching of Christ against the one who said, *I will sit in the sides of the north, I will be like the most High.*

St Augustine: Let us therefore hear the gospel just as if we were listening to the Lord himself present: nor let us say, 'O happy they who were able to see him!' Because there were many of them who saw, and also killed him; and there are many among us who have not seen him, and yet have believed. For the precious truth that sounded forth from the mouth of our Lord was both written for our sake, and preserved for our sake, and recited for our sake, and will be recited also for the sake of our posterity, even until the end of the world.

St Alphonsus: We should listen to the gospel as if were hearing the words of our divine Saviour instructing us himself, and we should at the same time ask him for the necessary help to put into practice what he teaches.

St Albert: When the gospel has been read, the deacon gives the gospel-book to the subdeacon to carry, to show that the latter has now been instructed. They return in procession to the giver of sanctity, to show that all good things must be referred to God. *Canst thou send lightning bolts, and will they go, and will they return and say* *to thee: Here we are?* Those who proclaim the gospel are lightning bolts who shine by their good examples and thunder with their words, and return to our Lord when they thank him for the progress they make. And the giver of sanctity kisses the book, that he may say with the Apostle, *I am delighted with the law of God, according to the inward man.* Thus ends the reading of the holy gospel, which is salvation for us, and defence against the devil.

CREDO

St Thomas Aquinas: Since we believe in Christ as in the divine truth – for he said, *If I say the truth to you, why do you not believe me?* – after the gospel has been read, the creed is sung. By this the people show that they give their assent, by faith, to Christ's doctrine.

St Albert: Someone might object: if this is so, the creed ought not to be begun by the giver of sanctity, the bishop or priest, but by one of the people, or at least by the choir. To this we reply that the giver of sanctity begins the creed to show that faith is a gift from God, and that from God through the givers of sanctity, good things flow in an orderly way through the various ranks of the Church to the people. As the psalmist says, *Like the precious ointment on the head, that ran down upon the beard, the beard of Aaron, which ran down to the skirt of his garments.*

St Robert Bellarmine: The custom of singing the creed at Mass is more ancient in the East than in the West. Among the Germans and the Gauls, the custom spread especially in the time of Charlemagne, who condemned the heresies of Felix, bishop of Urgel in the Pyrenees.

Dom Guéranger: Until the 11th century, the Creed was not publicly said in the churches at Rome. St Henry, Emperor of Germany, when visiting Rome, was surprised at not hearing the Creed during the Mass. The Pope told him that the Church at Rome showed in this way the purity of her faith: she had no need to express her rejection of errors which had never been harboured within her walls. However, shortly after the Emperor's remark, it was decided that the *Credo* should be said in the churches in Rome, on Sundays. For the confession of faith would become all the more solemn by being promulgated from the very Chair of St Peter.

St Albert: The Nicene Creed is only sung on solemn feast days which are mentioned within it. So it is sung on all Sundays, which celebrate the resurrection, and at the Nativity, and the Ascension and the feast of the Holy Ghost, and on their octave-days, for the eighth day is that of resurrection. It is also sung on feasts of our Lady, for she is mentioned in the Creed, and on feasts of the apostles, since we believe in the holy, Catholic and apostolic Church, and on the feast of the dedication of a Church, since we believe in the holy Church. Some also sing it on the feast of St Mary Magdalen, the apostle to the apostles, and on the feast of the Holy Cross, since we believe in him who was crucified.

St Thomas Aquinas: The Nicene Creed explains what is contained in the Apostles' Creed, and it was composed when the faith had already been publicly preached and when the Church had peace. This is why it is sung publicly at Mass. But the Apostles' Creed was composed during the time of persecution, before the faith had become public knowledge. This is why it is said in secret at Prime and Compline: a defence, as it were, against the darkness of past and future errors.

OFFERTORY
CHANT

St Thomas Aquinas: Now that the people have been prepared and instructed, the celebration of the mystery begins. This mystery is offered as a sacrifice and consecrated and received as a sacrament. So first comes an oblation; then the consecration of what has been offered; then the reception of this in the communion. The oblation consists in two things: the people's praise in the Offertory chant, which expresses the joy of those who offer, and the prayer of the priest, who asks that the people's oblation may be accepted by God. And so David says, *I also in the simplicity of my heart have joyfully offered all these things: and I have seen with great joy thy people which are here present, offer thee their offerings*; and then he prays, *Lord God, keep this will.*

Amalarius: From this point, all that is done in the Mass refers to what happened between that Palm Sunday when the children came to greet our Lord and the day of his ascension, or the day of Pentecost.

St Albert: The giver of sanctity turns to the people and says, *Dominus vobiscum.* 'May our Lord be with you, that you may be offered to God in sacrifice. May our Lord be with you, that you may feel the goodness of this oblation. May our Lord be with you, that you may be incorporated into the Sacrifice that is offered.'

Durandus: The priest turns to the people and then back to the altar, because Christ, when he lived here below, turned sometimes from prayer to preaching, and sometimes from preaching back to prayer.

Amalarius: He says, *Oremus,* and so counsels all present to enter into their consciences. If anyone has something to immolate, let him immolate it: that is, if anyone is conscious of guilt, let him ask that it may be slain by the unseen spear; if anyone has a voluntary sacrifice to offer, let him pray before it leaves his hand, so that it may be acceptable to our Lord.

St Albert: The outer oblation is the sign of an inner oblation, which must be made cheerfully and gladly; as it is said, *God loveth a cheerful giver.* For this reason, the Offertory chant should be sung to a lively and joyful melody.

St Isidore: The book of Ecclesiasticus witnesses that the ancients used to sing offertory chants when the victims were sacrificed, as we do in honour of our Sacrifice. For it says, *He stretched forth his hand to make a libation, and offered of the blood of the grape. Then the sons of Aaron shouted, they sounded with beaten trumpets, and made a great noise to be heard for a remembrance before God.* Likewise we, in answer to the trumpet, that is, the word of preaching, are enkindled by the chant, and rejoice to sing the praises of God by heart and mouth in this, the true sacrifice, by whose blood the whole world has been saved.

Amalarius: The cantors sing, following the example of the crowds who sang to Christ as he was coming to Jerusalem.

Strabo: It is not clearly recorded who first introduced this into our rite, as can also be said of the antiphon sung at Communion. It is thought, indeed, that at the earliest times the holy fathers offered and received communion in silence. Yet, as we have said, the beauty of the Church increases over the years by new means and new rites; nor will it cease to grow until the end.

OFFERTORY

Dom Guéranger: Having been immolated once on Calvary, he can do no more; yet, nevertheless, knowing what human weakness is, he feared lest the sacrifice of the Cross, only once offered, might at last make little impression on the faithful. Before long, man would have treated the sacrifice of Calvary as a mere historical fact, consigned to the pages of the Church's annals, where few even would think of seeking it. So our Lord said to himself, 'What was done once on Calvary must needs be renewed until the end of time.'

St John Fisher: For although Christ was offered once to take away all sins, yet sinners must by some suitable means be united with this offering, to receive its benefits.

St Justin Martyr: Bread is brought up, and wine and water, and the president sends up prayers and likewise thanksgivings.

St Robert Bellarmine: Five prayers are offered: *Suscipe, sancte Pater; Offerimus tibi Domine; Veni, Sanctificator; In spiritu humilitatis; Suscipe, sancta Trinitas.* They are not so very ancient; they have not been used by the Roman Church above five hundred years. But they have gradually come to be received by all.

St Alphonsus: In offering the bread and wine, the priest calls them *the immaculate host, the chalice of salvation*. We should not be astonished at this; for all the prayers and all the ceremonies before and after the consecration have reference to the divine victim. It is at the moment of consecration that the divine victim presents himself to God, that he offers himself to him, and that the sacrifice is offered; but as these different acts cannot be explained at the same time, they are explained one after the other.

St Jerome: The sacred chalices, veils and other accessories used in the celebration of our Lord's passion are not mere lifeless and senseless objects devoid of holiness. Rather, from their association with the body and blood of our Lord, they are to be venerated with the same awe as the body and blood themselves.

St Bede: *They took the body of Jesus and bound it in linen cloths*. Hence has come down the custom of the Church, of consecrating our Lord's body not on silk or gold, but in a clean linen cloth.

Remigius: Just as linen is made bright by wearisome labour, so Christ underwent many sufferings before he passed from this world to attain the brightness of the resurrection.

Amalarius: The fine cloth that we call the corporal admonishes the people and the ministers of the altar and also the priest: for just as that linen was worked on till it lost its natural greenness and moisture, so the minds of those who make the offering must be freed from all fleshly greed; and just as it is shining white, so they must shine in God's sight by the purity of their intention.

St Albert: We use the chalice to stand for the tomb, the paten for the stone placed at the mouth of the tomb, the pall and corporal for the winding cloths in which our Lord's body was wrapped by St Joseph in his work of love.

Durandus: The paten receives its name from the word *pateo*, to be wide open. For this reason it denotes a wide and generous heart. The sacrifice must be offered upon this paten, that is, with the breadth of charity. And because this generous charity failed the apostles when they all forsook their Master and fled, the priest conceals the paten when he has made the offering, placing it beneath the corporal; or else it is veiled by the subdeacon, and taken from the altar.

St Thomas Aquinas: The wine offered in this sacrament must be mixed with water. First, because this is how it was first instituted; for it is most probable that our Lord mixed water into the wine, according to the custom of his land. Secondly, because this is suitable for representing our Lord's passion.

St Paschasius: Blood and water flowed from the side of Christ when his passion was accomplished. The apostles understood this mystery, and ordained that it be done also in the chalice. In that way, nothing of those things done on the cross for our redemption would be lacking in this sacrament which commemorates the passion.

St Thomas Aquinas: Thirdly, this symbolizes the effect of the sacrament, the union of the Christian people with Christ.

St Cyprian: The divine scriptures declare in the Apocalypse that the waters signify the peoples. So when water is mixed with wine in the chalice, the people are united to Christ. Therefore in the sanctification of our Lord's chalice, neither wine alone nor water alone may be offered. If only wine were offered, then would the blood of Christ be without us. If there were only water, the people would be without Christ.

Durandus: The water is blessed, but the wine is not. Christ needs no blessing, but the people in this life cannot be without sin, and therefore they need God's blessing that they may be capable of this union with Christ.

St Thomas Aquinas: Fourthly, it befits the final effect of this sacrament, namely, entrance into eternal life. Hence Ambrose says, 'water falls into the chalice, and springs up to eternal life.'

Dom Guéranger: The wine represents Jesus Christ as God; the water represents him as man. The weakness of the water, compared with the strength of the wine, expresses the difference which between the humanity and the divinity of Jesus Christ. The Carthusians, who follow the liturgy of the eleventh century, and the Dominicans, who follow that of the thirteenth, do not perform this ceremony in the church; they do so in the sacristy, and sometimes at the altar, but always before commencing the Mass.

St Isidore: For in things not contrary to the faith or to good morals, we should follow and preserve the customs of those among whom we live, lest schisms should arise from variations in rite.

St Albert: The priest bows low before the altar, saying, *In a spirit of humility and in a contrite mind let us be received by thee, O Lord; and let our sacrifice be made such in thy sight this day that it may please thee, Lord God.* He asks that his work of sacrifice may be accepted because of the humility and contrition of the Church; and it is certain that what is offered in this way is never rejected.

St Robert Bellarmine: The priest does not doubt whether the sacrifice of the Mass will be pleasing to God in itself, or insofar as it was instituted by Christ; but he doubts of his own interior dispositions. For this reason, he asks for humility and contrition, that he may so continue the sacrifice which he has begun that it may also please God insofar as he is offering it.

St Thomas Aquinas: He joins his hands while bending low. This is the posture of one making humble supplication, and it represents the humility and obedience with which Christ suffered for us.

INCENSATION

St Albert: Incense was used in worship under the Old Law, and the Church has preserved this custom. For incense was not one of those things, like the paschal lamb, that merely foreshadowed something future, and so must no longer be observed. Rather, it signifies something that must always exist and always be renewed: the pleasure with which we devote ourselves to God in prayer and sacrifice.

St Thomas Aquinas: We do not use incense as if we were following the ceremonies commanded by the Old Law, but because this custom has been ordained by the Church. It is used, first, out of reverence for the sacrament, since its sweet smell blots out any physical stench that might be present in the place, which would be repellent. Next, it serves to represent the effect of grace. For Christ was full of grace, as of a sweet smell, according to the prophecy of Jacob, *Behold, the smell of my son is as the smell of a plentiful field*. This grace passes to the faithful through the work of Christ's ministers. So St Paul says, *He sprinkles the odour of his knowledge by us in every place*. For this reason, first the altar, which represents Christ, is incensed completely, then all present are incensed in order of rank.

Dom Guéranger: Before making use of the incense, it must be blessed; the priest does so by the following prayer: *Through the intercession of blessed Michael the archangel, standing at the right of the altar of incense* . . . The angel who holds the golden thurible in the Apocalypse is not named. Holy Church here names St Michael, prince of the heavenly hosts. Some have thought that there is an error in this passage, because in Saint Luke, the angel Gabriel is named standing at the right of the altar; but holy Church pays no heed to these objections.

Amalarius: The thurible with which he incenses the offerings shows through whom propitiation will be made for him to God. It will be made through our Lord Jesus Christ, of whose body the thurible is a symbol.

St Robert Bellarmine: Incense is used because of the likeness that it has to prayer. So it is said in the psalm, *Let my prayer be directed as incense in thy sight*. It is also used to represent the glory of God, for in the Old Testament he often showed himself in a cloud.

Durandus: The prayers of the saints bring us to an eternal crown through the burning charity of our Lord's passion, and so the priest swings the censer both in the shape of a cross and of a crown.

St Vincent Ferrer: When you smell that pleasant odour of incense, you should think how Christ suffered for us so patiently, and how sweet was the scent of his soul's sacrifice before God and the holy angels in heaven and the holy fathers in Limbo.

Durandus: He incenses the offerings with threefold swings, to recall how Mary Magdalene thrice brought spices to anoint the body of Jesus. Once, when she anointed his feet at the house of Simon the Pharisee; once when she poured ointment upon his head in the house of Simon the leper; and once when she went with spices to anoint Jesus after he had been placed in the tomb – for there the intention is counted for the deed. And he goes on to incense the altar on every side, since the fame of that deed has been spread throughout the Church, as our Lord himself foretold.

LAVABO

St Albert: Next comes the washing of the hands. For although the celebrant has already washed himself from iniquity when he was preparing for Mass, yet now that he is about to offer the sacrifice, he needs a further cleansing from venial sins and from the remnants of past sins. David sought this further cleansing when he said, *Wash me yet more from my iniquity* – as if to say, 'thou hast washed me from mortal sins; wash me also from venial.'

St Cyril of Jerusalem: We did not set out for the church with defiled hands; this washing is a symbol that you ought to be pure from all sinful and unlawful deeds. For since the hands are a symbol of action, by washing them we represent the purity and blamelessness of our conduct. Or have you not heard how blessed David disclosed this mystery, saying, *I will wash my hands among the innocent; and will compass thy altar, O Lord.*

St Thomas Aquinas: The washing of extremities signifies a washing even from the smallest sins, according to the words, *He that is washed needeth not but to wash his feet.*

Dionysius: For it behoves those who approach that most hallowed service to be purified even to the remotest imaginations of the soul.

St Thomas Aquinas: This was also signified by the washing of the priests under the Old Law. Yet the Church has not preserved it as if she were following a ceremonial regulation of the Old Law, but as something she herself has instituted, and as something intrinsically fitting. For this reason, it is not done in the same way now as then. The washing of the feet is omitted and the washing of the hands is preserved. This is simpler and yet serves to express complete purification, since the hand is the 'organ of organs'.

ORATE, FRATRES

St Albert: Now he turns to the people, asking them to support him by their prayer in the unity of the Church, saying, *Pray, brethren, that my sacrifice and yours may be acceptable before God the Father almighty.* Even though he holds the place of the giver of sanctity, he seeks the help of prayer, to show the truth of the Apostle's words, *He himself also is compassed with infirmity.* And the infirm man needs the help of the Church, for St James says, *Pray for one another, that you may be saved.*

Blessed Columba Marmion: The priest invites the faithful and the heavenly spirits to surround the altar that is about to become a new Calvary, and to accompany the holy action with praise and homage.

St Leonard: Those who hear Mass are not only present at it but also offer it, and have themselves a right to the title of priests: *Thou hast made us to our God a kingdom and priests.* Therefore the priest turns round to the people and says, *Pray, brethren, that my sacrifice and yours may be acceptable,* in order that the faithful may understand that while he indeed is the principal minister, all those present make the great offering with him.

St Alphonsus: It must be observed that there is a great difference between sacrificing and offering. To the priest alone belongs the right to sacrifice, whereas all those who are present may offer the sacrifice.

St Albert: He says, 'mine and yours', for both what is offered on the altar and those who offer it are offered to God. And by giving of their substance that the offering may be made, the people manifest their interior oblation to God.

St Thomas Aquinas: The priest turns to the people five times in the course of the Mass. This signifies that our Lord showed himself five times on the day of the Resurrection.

St Bonaventure: This third time that he turns to the people, he speaks silently. This represents the appearance made to Peter, of which it is nowhere told when or how it took place.

Durandus: On this occasion, after the priest has spoken these words, he completes the circle in turning back to the altar. For one psalm says, *I have gone round and have offered up a sacrifice of jubilation*. So he does indeed go round, as he prepares himself to sacrifice.

Dom Guéranger: These words form the priest's farewell to the people, for he will not again turn to them, until the sacrifice be achieved.

SECRET

St Albert: Now the giver of sanctity offers the secret prayer. At every Mass throughout the year he asks that the people who have offered their gifts may be incorporated into the body of Christ and so offered to God. This is made clear by the secret prayer of the first Mass of the year:[16] *May these sacred things, O Lord, cleanse us by their mighty power, and make us come in purity to their origin.* For the origin of these offerings is the offering that Christ made of himself. This prayer is called the Secret because it is said silently and secretly. The reason for this is that the giver of sanctity is now offering and asking for the holiest of things, and these must be concealed from the mass of people, so that they may be reverenced the more. For things that are shown to the people become familiar and are reckoned of little worth.

St Thomas Aquinas: Some things in the Mass, the priest says publicly, namely the common prayers that pertain both to himself and to the people. Other things pertain only to the priest, such as the offering and the consecration, and so these are said in secret. Yet in

---

16. That is, the Mass of the first Sunday in Advent.

each, he stirs up the attention of the people, beginning *Dominus vobiscum*, and waiting for the *Amen*.

St Albert: There is a sign of this in the Book of Numbers, where Aaron and his priest sons alone must enter the tabernacle and sort and carry the things when the camp is to advance. None other of the people are allowed to see the things of the sanctuary before they have been wrapped up; and if they look out of curiosity, they must die. For many people despise holy things which are put publicly on display, and so they take from them an occasion of death; but if they had been covered and wrapped up and veiled from their sight, they would have revered them.

Amalarius: Christ was the paschal lamb prepared for sacrifice, though this lay hid. It was concealed from the apostles; it was concealed from the others who believed; it was concealed from the people of the Jews, until the day of the Supper, when he manifested the passion more clearly. Therefore the priest speaks in secret until that day arrives.

PREFACE DIALOGUE

The Lord be with you
And with thy spirit.

Be your hearts on high.
We have them with the Lord.

Let us give thanks to the
Lord our God.
It is fitting and just.

St Albert: Hearing the people's 'Amen', the priest perceives that they are now prepared for higher things, and so he speaks to them publicly of the greatness and sacredness of this sacrament. He greets them, saying *Dominus vobiscum*, for without our Lord we cannot attain these heights. We gladly reply, *Et cum spiritu tuo*, asking that the priest's spirit may be with the Spirit who makes holiness perfect. And this is most necessary in this sacrament, in which the flesh is of no avail, and the spirit works all things.

St Thomas Aquinas: The priest greets the people seven times in the Mass, five when he turns to them, and twice without turning, namely before the Preface and when he says, *Pax Domini sit semper vobiscum*. This denotes the sevenfold grace of the Holy Ghost.

St John Chrysostom: If the Holy Spirit were not present

in him who is our common father and teacher, you would not all have replied with one voice, *And with thy spirit.* Hence, you do not only pronounce this word when he ascends to the altar or when he is conversing with you or praying for you, but also when he stands before the Holy Table, about to offer the awesome sacrifice. Your words recall to your mind that he who is present does nothing of himself; it is the grace of the Spirit who has descended upon all which alone accomplishes the mystic sacrifice. Yes, a man is there; but God is acting through him.

Amalarius: Now that the priest is occupied at the altar, it is more fitting for him to remain as he is than to look behind him, for thus he expresses the inner devotion with which he offers the sacrifice. The ploughman must not turn and look back when he is performing his worthy action. Nor would it be right for one who wishes to praise our Lord to turn his back to him, and his breast to servants.

St Thomas Aquinas: Now the consecration of this sacrament is a work of supernatural power. So the people are first incited to devotion, and admonished in the Preface to hold their hearts on high before our Lord.

St Vincent Ferrer: The Mass is the highest work of contemplation that can be. And so the priest raises his hands, as to fly, and he says, *Hearts on high.* And the people reply, 'We are already holding them before our Lord.'

St Cyprian: When we stand praying, beloved brethren, we ought to be watchful and earnest with our whole heart, intent on our prayers. Let all carnal and worldly thoughts pass away, nor let the soul at that time think on anything but the object only of its prayer. For this reason also the priest by way of preface before his prayer, prepares the minds of the brethren by saying, *Lift up your hearts*, that so upon the people's response, *We have them before our Lord*, he may be reminded that he himself ought to think of nothing but our Lord.

St Cyril of Jerusalem: Let no one come here, who with his lips can say, *We lift up our hearts to our Lord*, but in his mind employs his thoughts on worldly business. God indeed should be in our memory at all times, but if this is impossible because of human infirmity, at least in this hour this should be our earnest endeavour.

St Augustine: The action that is mentioned in the sacraments of the faithful, that we should lift up our hearts to our Lord, is itself a gift from him. After these words, the faithful are admonished to give thanks to the Lord our God for this gift, and they reply that it is right and just. For since our heart is not in our own power, but is lifted up by the help of God so that it may rise upward and taste *not the things that are on earth but the things which are above, where Christ is seated at the right hand of God*, to whom ought we to give thanks for this great benefit, if not to the Lord our God?'

St Cyril of Jerusalem: You say, *It is fitting and just*; for in giving thanks we do something fitting and just, but he did something more than just when he did us good and counted us fit for such great benefits.

Dom Guéranger: This dialogue is as old as the Church herself; and there is every reason to believe that the Apostles themselves arranged it, because it is to be found in the most ancient Churches and in all liturgies.

PREFACE

It is truly fitting and just, right and salutary, that we should always and everywhere give thanks to thee, O holy Lord, Father almighty, eternal God, through Christ our Lord.
Through whom the angels praise thy majesty, the dominations adore it, and the powers are in awe; the heavens and the virtues of heaven and the blessed seraphim celebrate with great joy.
With these, we pray thee, command that even our voices may be joined, while we say with lowly praise:

St Robert Bellarmine: The preface is so called because it prepares and stirs up the people in readiness for that action in which the sacrifice properly speaking consists. The words that precede the *Sanctus* are not the same in the Greek and Latin liturgy. Yet what is done in the liturgy of the Roman Church is certainly very ancient. For a thousand years ago, Pope Pelagius was asked by the bishops of France and Germany how many authentic prefaces there were, and he replied that there were nine: of the Nativity, Epiphany, Lent, the Cross, Easter, Ascension, Pentecost, the Trinity and the Apostles. Pope Urban added a tenth preface in the year

1080; this is the preface of the Blessed Virgin.

St Albert: To approve the people's answer, he says, *It is truly fitting and just, right and salutary.* Under the old Law, nothing fit to be offered to God was found. So the Apocalypse expresses the laments of the ancient Fathers who did not possess this sacrifice: *I wept much, because no man was found worthy to open the book, nor to see it.* The book is the secret plan of the divine wisdom, which was to make the Church strong and beautiful with the sacraments. And no one could open this but him who made the sacraments flow forth from his heart by his blood.

Dom Guéranger: All prefaces are formed on the one great idea of giving thanks to God, and of making this thanksgiving *through Jesus Christ,* because it is by him alone that we can come nigh unto God, yea, approach him in union with the angels.

St John Chrysostom: Continual thanksgiving is the sure guardian of all God's graces. For this reason our awesome and saving mysteries, celebrated wherever the Church gathers, are called *eucharistia,* that is, thanksgiving.

St Albert: Thanks must be given *always and everywhere* for this great sacrament. *Always,* that is, both in the time of grace and in the eternity of glory. *Everywhere,* because through this sacrament things in heaven and things on earth are restored. Creation's three-fold frame gives thanks when this sacrament is offered: heaven, because the fall of the angels is made good; earth, for the militant Church is redeemed; the underworld, for those detained therein are freed. They must be given *through Christ our Lord,* for as a canal touches the fountain from which it springs and the garden which it waters, so our Emmanuel by his divinity touches God from whom the gifts of grace come and by his humanity he touches us into whom they flow through him. Therefore we give thanks through Christ magnificently.

Dom Guéranger: The Preface is intoned on the very same melody used by the ancient Greeks when celebrating some hero in their feasts, and there declaiming his mighty deeds in song.

St Albert: God shows his majesty above all by this, that though incomprehensible, he encloses himself in something so small; that received as food, he remains in himself unchanging; that reigning in eternity, he is mystically slain upon the altar. *Who hath ever heard such a thing? And who hath ever seen the like to this?* And so *the angels praise* the power of God, which has triumphed over the enemy by this sacrifice.

St John Chrysostom: He names the cherubim and the seraphim, then he exhorts us to join our voices with theirs, in that song full of a holy fear. It is as if he is saying to each of us, 'Since you sing with the seraphim, stand erect like the seraphim, spread your wings as they do, fly with them about the royal throne.'

St Albert: *With these we pray thee,* for without thy help our voice may never be heard among the angels, *command*, O God, giver of all holiness, *that even our voices*, which though lowly are yet rational, *may be joined, while we say with lowly praise*, prostrate before thy majesty, the hymn that the holy angels sing, as Isaias told.

Durandus: The preface may also represent how Jesus went to the great upper room that had been made ready for the Passover, where he spoke much with the disciples and giving thanks, sang a hymn to God the Father. *And a hymn being said, they went out unto mount Olivet.*

SANCTUS

Holy, holy, holy,
Lord God of Sabaoth.
The heavens and the earth are full of thy glory:
Hosanna in the highest. Blessed is he that cometh in
the name of the Lord. Hosanna in the highest.

St Vincent Ferrer: The King does not come alone. The holy angels are at the altar in Christ's company, singing, 'The bread of angels becomes the bread of men.'

St Clement of Rome: Scripture says, 'Ten thousand times ten thousand stood before him, and thousands of thousands ministered to him, and they cried, "Holy, holy, holy Lord of hosts, the whole creation is full of his glory."' We too, therefore, gathering together in one accord in our conscience, should cry out earnestly as with one voice to him.

St John Chrysostom: Do you recognise these words? Are they ours, or the seraphim's? They are both ours and the seraphim's, since Christ has raised the partition that separated these two worlds. He has made peace to reign on earth and in heaven; he has made of the two things one.

St Thomas Aquinas: With the angels, the people devoutly praise the divinity of Christ, saying *Sanctus,*

Sanctus, Sanctus. With the children they praise his humanity, saying, *Benedictus qui venit*.

St Antoninus: *Sanctus* is said thrice, to express the mystery of the Trinity of persons. But to express the unity of the essence, *Dominus Deus* is said.

St Albert: It may also be said thrice because this sacrament is composed of three things, one ancient, one new, one eternal. First, the matter of Christ's body, which came from the ancient stock of Adam, though sanctified by the Holy Spirit. Second, his human soul that was created from nothing by the Father and filled with all holiness and grace and wisdom. Third, his deity, which joined to itself the holy body and soul in the person of the Son. *The heavens* are full of his glory because those whom this sacrifice commemorates and praises are triumphant in beatitude. *The earth* means those who dwell and do battle upon the earth, for whom this sacrifice is offered as help and food. It means too those suffering punishment under the earth, for whom it is offered as a prayer. *Sabaoth* means 'of powers' or 'of armies'. For to the devil, the holy Church militant and triumphant is *terrible as an army set in array*.

St John Chrysostom: These words show us the divinity of Christ. *Hosanna* is 'save us' – and salvation in the Scriptures is attributed to God alone. And *he comes*, it is said, not 'he is brought': the former befits a lord, the latter a servant.

St Bede: 'In the name of the Lord' signifies, 'in the name of God the Father'. As he said elsewhere to the Jews who did not believe, *I am come in the name of my*

Father and you receive me not. If another shall come in his own name, him you will receive. Christ came in the name of God the Father because in everything that he did and said he was concerned with glorifying his Father, and with proclaiming to men that he is to be glorified. Antichrist will come in his own name, for *he opposeth and is lifted up above all that is called God, or that is worshipped.*

St Albert: *Hosanna* is said again, that the one who saved us from one wretchedness by grace may save us from another wretchedness by glory. And *in excelsis* is added again, for none may reach either the heights of glory or the heights of grace, save by him.

Dom Guéranger: Truly, the Jews did well to shout their *Hosanna,* as they went, wending in glad procession down the mount of Olives, towards Jerusalem, entering by the Golden Gate; all was in harmony, and breathed triumph; but how far more fitting is it for us to sing it, at this portentous moment, when the Son of God is about to come down in the midst of us who truly know him!

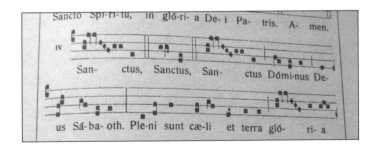

THE ROMAN CANON

Council of Trent: Since holy things must be treated in a holy way, and this sacrifice is of all things the most holy, the Catholic Church instituted many centuries ago the sacred Canon, so that this sacrifice might be offered and understood in a worthy and reverent way. It is so pure from error, that there is nothing in it but what breathes forth the greatest holiness and devotion and raises up to God the minds of those who offer. For it is made from the very words of our Lord, the traditions of the apostles, and the devout ordinance of holy pontiffs.

St Robert Bellarmine: The first to give to the Roman Church a form of celebrating the sacrifice was undoubtedly St Peter, who added to the words of our Lord certain prayers and rites. After him, various Pontiffs added various prayers until the time of Pope Gregory, who was the last to add anything to the Canon. It is most impressive and admirable that the prayers of the Canon, though composed by several authors, should fit so aptly together that but one man seems responsible for the whole.

Dom Guéranger: The various prayers of which the Canon is composed are of the highest antiquity; nevertheless, they cannot be traced to the very first days of holy Church. This is proved by the fact that divine worship was first performed in the Greek tongue, a language in much more general use at that epoch than Latin. It is probable, therefore, to suppose that the prayers as we have them were drawn up in the second century, or possibly as late as the first years of the third.

St Robert Bellarmine: Our opponents find fault with the Latin Church that she commands many things in the Mass to be spoken in a low voice. Now there is no dispute about whether it would be unlawful to say the whole Mass in a normal voice. We know well that the level of the voice is not an essential part of the sacrifice, and that such things can be changed by the judgement of the Church. But the Council of Trent defined that it is not contrary to Christ's intention that some things should be said in a low voice, and many considerations show how true this is. First, it promotes the reverence due to so great a sacrament.

St Basil: Why did the great Moses determine that not everything in the temple would be accessible to all? In his wisdom, he knew well that those things may be easily despised to which we have access straightaway and constantly; but that an object that is rare and set apart excites interest. In the same way, the apostles and the fathers who set the churches in order in the beginning protected the sacred character of the Mysteries by silence and concealment.

St Cyprian: When we meet together with the brethren in one place, and celebrate divine sacrifices with God's priest, we ought to be mindful of modesty and discipline – not to throw abroad our prayers indiscriminately, with voices unsubdued, nor to cast to God with tumultuous wordiness a petition that ought to be commended to God by modesty. Anna, who was a type of the Church, observed this when she prayed to God not with clamorous petition, but silently and modestly, within the very recesses of her heart. Divine Scripture asserts, *Anna spoke in her heart, and only her lips moved, but her voice was not heard*; and God heard her.

St Robert Bellarmine: We also have the example of the sacrifices of the old Law. For in the solemn offering of the incense, it was commanded that only the priest should pass through the veil to sacrifice, praying for himself and for the people. They stood without, waiting, and not only did they not hear the priest, they could not even see him. This was the rite by which Zachary, father of the Precursor, offered sacrifice. Again, when Christ hung upon the cross, as the exemplar of all sacrifices, he made his oblation in silence. In the space of three hours he spoke only seven brief words to the bystanders. And seven sentences are spoken aloud in our Canon too.[17]

---

17. The author must here be understanding the term 'canon' in a wide sense, perhaps to refer to the whole sacrificial act from the offertory to the priest's communion. Thus understood, the priest would break the silence on seven occasions: at the *Orate fratres*, at the end of the Secret prayer, at the *nobis quoque peccatoribus*, at the end of the canon in the strict sense, at the end of the embolism, at the *Agnus Dei*, at the *Domine, non sum dignus*.

Durandus: Human reason can by no means obtain a full understanding of this great mystery, and this is well signified by its being offered in a low voice. The Canon is also recited quietly lest the priest, in speaking loudly of what he is doing, should think about it the less. It must be said briskly, not slowly, lest the hearers grow weary. So it was said concerning the immolation of the lamb, *Do it in haste*. Yet it should not be too hurried, since no sacrifice should be offered without salt, that is, without care and devotion. Again, he prays silently so that he may pray with more devotion, not thinking whether his voice or his manner is being admired by the people; also, because our Lord in the garden withdrew from his disciples about the space of a stone's throw so that he might pray.

Amalarius: Christ sought for solitude in his prayer: and how much more must not we seek this, who are pressed hard on every side by the crowds of vices and by our worldly habits!

Ven. John Henry Newman: Words are necessary, but as means, not as ends; they are not mere addresses to the throne of grace, they are instruments of what is far higher, of consecration, of sacrifice. They hurry on as if impatient to fulfil their mission. Quickly they go, the whole is quick, for they are all parts of one integral action. Quickly they go, for they are awful words of sacrifice, they are a work too great to delay upon; as when it was said in the beginning, 'What thou doest, do quickly.' Quickly they pass, for the Lord Jesus goes with them, as he passed along the lake in the days of his flesh, calling first one and then another. Quickly they pass; because as the lightning which shineth from one part of the heaven unto the other, so is the coming of the Son of Man.

St Vincent Ferrer: Someone may say, 'and I, who belong to the people of God, and am a sheep of his pasture, what shall I do? How shall I occupy myself?' With divine praises, with the *Pater Noster,* the *Ave Maria*, the psalms.

St Francis de Sales: After the *Sanctus*, think with all humility and reverence of the great blessing of the death and passion of our Saviour; ask him to bring it to all the world, especially to the children of the Church and to those who are close to us. Ask him that it may be for the glory and happiness of the saints in heaven, and a solace for the souls in Purgatory.

St Leonard: Some read nothing whatever during the divine sacrifice, but fix their mental eye, kindled by faith, on Jesus crucified, and leaning against the tree of the cross, gather its fruits in contemplation. And such as these, keeping their faculties gathered up in God, will arrive at heroic acts of faith, hope and charity.

ROMAN CANON: TE IGITUR

We therefore humbly pray and beseech thee, most merciful Father, through Jesus Christ thy Son our Lord, that thou wouldst deign to accept and bless these ✠ gifts, these ✠ offerings, these ✠ holy and unspotted sacrifices: which in the first place we offer thee for thy holy catholic church; deign to grant her peace, to protect, unite and govern her throughout the whole world; together with thy servant, our Pope N., our bishop N., and all orthodox believers and worshippers of the catholic and apostolic faith.

Remigius: When praise and thanksgiving have been made for the great grace of our redemption, then comes a silence upon all the Church. The noise of words stops: the heart's devotion attends to God alone: and the priest, accompanied by the prayers and desires of all, begins to pour forth the prayer.

St Robert Bellarmine: This part of the Mass is also called the *Action*, for the action of the sacrifice is celebrated within it; the other parts of the Mass are rather words than actions.

St Thomas Aquinas: The priest secretly commemorates, first, those for whom this sacrifice is offered,
that is, the universal Church and those *that are in high
station*, and then in particular those who are offering
and those for whom it is offered.

St Albert: He continues from what was said in the
Sanctus. 'Since the giver of all sanctity is holy in the
unity of the Trinity, and all heaven and earth are filled
with thy glory by this sacrament, *therefore we pray*; for
thou hast given us cause and reason to pray by filling
heaven and earth with thy glory through the sacrifice.'

Dom Guéranger: The initial letter of the first prayer
of the Canon is T, which by its very shape, represents a
cross. No other sign could better be placed as a heading
to this great prayer, in the course of which the sacrifice
of Calvary is renewed.

Amalarius: Those behind the priest remain bowed down
throughout this prayer. For these are the apostles who were
oppressed by great trouble at the time of the passion; nor
did they dare to stand up straight and confess themselves
Christ's disciples until the resurrection of our Lord.

St Robert Bellarmine: Luther objects that before
the consecration the bread and wine are called *holy
and unspotted sacrifices*. But they can rightly be so called.
Sacrifices, because they are the matter for the sacrifice,
and already prepared and dedicated so that the sacrifice
will come from them. *Holy and unspotted*, because they
are consecrated to divine use by the offering which has
gone before, and because the Church offers them with
a pure and holy intention.

St Antoninus: They are called *unspotted*, that is, incorrupt, both because of the matter of this sacrament, which must be worthy, and because of what they are to contain, that is, the body of Christ, and because of the mystical body of Christ that is thereby signified.

St Albert: The *gifts, offerings and sacrifices* are at the same time those who offer, the things that they offer, and the one who will be offered in them to the Father. And the sign of the Cross is made three times to represent this triple distinction.

St Thomas Aquinas: The priest uses the sign of the Cross when celebrating the Mass to express the passion of Christ, which was completed on the Cross. Now Christ's passion was accomplished in various stages. First, he was handed over. Now this was done by God, by Judas, and by the Jews, and the priest symbolises this by the triple sign of the Cross at the words, *these ✠ gifts, these ✠ offerings, these ✠ holy and unspotted sacrifices.*

Durandus: Or, These crosses are made to recall the triple crucifixion. The first was done in the hearts of those who persecuted him, of which it is said, *Then were gathered together the chief priests and ancients of the people, and they consulted together that by subtility they might apprehend Jesus and put him to death.* The second was in the voices of those who made the clamour, of which it is said, *They cried out the more: Crucify him.* The third was the crucifixion of his hands and his feet.

St Peter Damian: For in the Canon of the Mass, the words declare one thing, and the signs declare another.

The words principally concern the Eucharist that is consecrated, but the signs refer to the past events being recalled.

Dom Guéranger: The first interest at stake, when Mass is said, is holy Church, than which nothing is dearer to God; he cannot fail to be touched, when his Church is spoken of.

St Robert Bellarmine: When we say that we offer bread to God on behalf of the Church, the meaning is that we offer it to him to be consecrated, so that by this consecration a true sacrifice may be immolated to God for the sake of the Church.

St Augustine: This Church is Israel according to the spirit. For Israel according to the flesh served the sacrificial shadows which prefigured the one sacrifice now offered by Israel according to the spirit.

St Robert Bellarmine: Then the pope is named, then the bishop of the place.

Blessed Hyacinth Cormier: Jesus himself encourages us to show this act of devotion to the pope, saying to St Peter, *I have prayed for thee.*

St Albert: For although the pope and bishops are set in authority over men, and so take the place of the giver of sanctity, yet they are themselves frail men. Therefore they require prayers, and more indeed than other men. For the more the Church relies on them, the more they need the help of grace. Also, the devil plots against them more than against others. *Her enemies are at her head, her enemies are enriched.*

St Robert Bellarmine: Then he names the king, in certain churches, then all who are orthodox.

St Albert: This means, all who hold the true and sound doctrine of the faith, according to the words, *And whosoever shall follow this rule, peace on them, and mercy, and upon the Israel of God.*

St Antoninus: *Orthodox* means 'rightly glorifying'. So he is orthodox who glorifies God by the confession of the right faith.

St Albert: All who worship in this faith belong to the city of the Church, that is, to the unity of the Church's citizens, and so prayer must be made for all of them during the oblation. *Seek the peace of the city to which I have caused you to be carried away; and pray to the Lord for it: for in the peace thereof shall be your peace.*

St Thomas Aquinas: This sacrifice, which is the memorial of our Lord's passion, only benefits those who are united to this sacrament in faith and charity. For this reason, we do not pray in the Canon of the Mass for those who are outside the Church.[18] And yet, even if someone does not yet possess a spiritual life, this sacrifice can be offered for him for as long as he still has the capacity to possess one. So it is true that 'the body of Christ is only offered for the members of Christ': but it is also said to be offered for his members when it is offered that someone may become one.

---

18. This does not exclude the priest's silently praying for such a person at the *Memento* of the living.

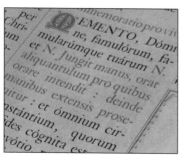

ROMAN CANON: MEMENTO OF THE LIVING

Be mindful, O Lord, of thy servants and handmaids, N. and N., and of all here present whose faith and devotion are known to thee: for whom we offer, or who offer up to thee, this sacrifice of praise for themselves and theirs; for the redemption of their souls, for the hope of their safety and salvation, and who pay their vows to thee, the eternal, true and living God.

St Albert: The first kind of communion is that which comes from obedience and authority, and which we have with the nobler members of the Church, such as the pope, patriarchs, and bishops. Here he speaks of the second form of communion in the mystical body, by which any member shares in what is beneficial to any other member.

St Robert Bellarmine: Zwingli does not approve of the phrase, *Be mindful O Lord, of thy servants*, saying, 'We seem to fear that God might be forgetful, so that we should have to bring something to his attention.' But he seems to have forgotten how Scripture speaks, or if does remember, he must be desirous of correcting the Holy Ghost – for what occurs more often in Scripture that *Be mindful*, or *Remember, O Lord*. What seems even more remarkable, we read in Scripture, *Do not forget*, and *Why do you forget?* In reality, God is said by a metaphor to forget when he does not help, and to remember when he begins to help.

Blessed Hyacinth Cormier: A teacher of grammar used an unusual method in deciding who to pray for here, taken from the declension of the noun. Nominative: pray for oneself. Genitive: pray for our parents who engendered us and for all our family, or for the pastors of the Church, who engender Jesus Christ in us each day. Dative: pray for those who have given us their help. Accusative: pray for those who have accused us or are hostile to us. Vocative: pray for those who have invoked our prayers. Ablative: Pray for those who have withdrawn themselves from the communion of the Church and her graces, by unbelief, or by disordered lives.

St Leonard: You will, perhaps, say to me, 'It suffices to hear one single Mass to strike off the heaviest debts due to God through many committed sins, because, Mass being of infinite value, we can therewith pay to God an infinite debt.' Not so fast, by your leave; because although indeed Mass is of infinite value, you must know nevertheless, that Almighty God accepts it in a manner limited and finite, and in degrees conformable to the greater or lesser perfections in the dispositions of him who celebrates or assists at the sacrifice. *Whose faith and devotion are known to thee*, says holy Church, suggesting by this manner of speech that the greater or less satisfaction applied in our behalf by the sacrifice is determined by the higher or lower dispositions of the celebrant and of those present.

St Thomas Aquinas: Compared to the other sacraments, this sacrament requires both a greater and a more widespread devotion. Devotion must be greater, since the whole Christ is contained in this sacrament, and more widespread, for while the other sacraments require devotion only on the part of those who receive them, this requires the devotion of the whole Christian people, for whom the sacrifice is offered.

Dom Guéranger: As for those who are absent, they too can participate of the sacrifice, by uniting themselves spiritually thereto and by desiring to assist thereat with faith and devotion, were it in their power to come.

St Robert Bellarmine: The *sacrifice of praise* is not the spiritual sacrifice that consists of praise and thanksgiving, but the sacrifice of the true body of our Lord. This is called a sacrifice of praise, because God is greatly praised thereby, and thanks are given unto him for the great blessings shown to us.

St Albert: The psalmist says, *The sacrifice of praise shall glorify me: and there is the way by which I will shew him the salvation of God.* For the way to salvation has never passed through any sacrifice but this.

St Robert Bellarmine: We should note that redemption in Scripture has five senses, and that those who have been redeemed in one sense may still need to be redeemed in others. It means in the first place being redeemed from all the evil of guilt and punishment by the payment of a sufficient price, and in this sense, all men have been redeemed by the Cross of Christ. Next, it means being redeemed from guilt by the application of the ransom paid on the Cross; and many are still in need of this kind of redemption. Thirdly, it means redemption from an outstanding debt of punishment, and often those who are redeemed in the first two ways still need this redemption. Again, it can mean redemption from future sins, for God is said to redeem those whom he preserves from sins into which they would otherwise have fallen. Finally, redemption is from corruption and from all the pains of this life, which will take place at the last resurrection. And all men, however holy they are, need these last two forms of redemption. The first redemption is not achieved by the Mass, since it was accomplished upon the Cross, though it is represented and applied by the Mass. But for all the other kinds of redemption, the Mass is of no small benefit, and so it is not surprising if the Mass is said to be offered for the redemption of the faithful.

St Albert: Two things are sought for the body. We ask that the sick may be made well and become strong for God's service, just as our Lord healed the bodies of many. And we pray for the *soundness* of the healthy, by the offering of this oblation, since health cannot continue unless God preserves it.

St Leonard: The Mass calls down temporal blessings, insofar as these do not oppose the salvation of the soul, such as health, abundance, peace, with the exclusion of the evils which are their opposites, such as pestilences, earthquakes, wars, famines, persecutions, hatreds, calumnies and injuries.

St Robert Bellarmine: For if this sacrifice can propitiate God and restore his enemies to his friendship, how much more readily will it induce him to give temporal blessings to his friends and those who have been reconciled to him, if these will be profitable for them.

Durandus: Or, he prays for the safety of the body and the salvation of the soul: for each form of health comes from him who said, *I am the salvation of the people.*

St Robert Bellarmine: Chemnitz objects to the words, *who pay their vows to thee,* saying that this refers to votive Masses which are celebrated in return for money. But this is a calumny. By *vows,* the Canon understands the holy desires and self-offering of the people present; and these words are said at all masses, whether votive Masses or not, and by priests who never accept any money in return for the celebration of Mass.

ROMAN CANON: COMMUNICANTES

In communion and venerating in the first place the memory of the glorious Mary, ever a virgin, mother of our God and Lord, Jesus Christ: as also of blessed Joseph, spouse of the same Virgin; and of thy blessed apostles and martyrs, Peter and Paul, Andrew, James, John, Thomas, James, Philip, Bartholomew, Matthew, Simon and Thaddaeus, Linus, Cletus, Clement, Xystus, Cornelius, Cyprian, Laurence, Chrysogonus, John and Paul, Cosmas and Damian, and of all thy saints: by whose merits and prayers grant that we may be defended in all things by thy protecting help. Through the same Christ our Lord. Amen.

St Albert: Here the Canon comes to the third form of communion, which is more hidden than the other two. Therefore, it expressly states that we are in communion with the saints in heaven by the sacrament of the altar: for what they see in plain truth, we approach through the appearance of the sacrament.

St Alphonsus: We who are travellers on earth form only one body with the saints who are in heaven, and united with them in the same spirit, we offer to God the same sacrifice.

St Robert Bellarmine: Those who have preceded us have explained this term *Communicantes* in two ways. Some refer it to our communion with the saints, so that the sense would be 'We offer this sacrifice in communion with the saints whom we remember, and we venerate these same saints.' Others refer it to the communion which those who offer the Mass have among themselves, so that the sense would be, 'We offer it while being in communion, that is, united among ourselves as befits the members of one body; and moreover, we venerate the memory of the saints.' For at Christmas, Epiphany, Easter, Ascension and Pentecost, after the word *Communicantes,* there is added *and celebrating the sacred day,* and a little later, *and also venerating the memory etc.*

St Albert: She is mentioned *in the first place* who is rightly always put first, the glorious ever-virgin Mary. Afterwards come *the blessed apostles,* who were the founders and preachers of our faith. As it is said in the psalms, *The foundations thereof are in the holy mountains,* the mountains *whence help shall come to me.*

St Antoninus: He mentions the Virgin, who offered Christ in the temple; the apostles, who handed down to us the rite of offering; and the martyrs, who offered themselves to God. But he does not mention the confessors, either because Mass was not offered in their honour in the most ancient days, or because they did not suffer in the same way as Christ, the memory of whose sufferings is here recalled.

St Robert Bellarmine: A sign of the antiquity of the Canon is that the apostles are not enumerated in the same order as in any of the gospels. This indicates that this part of the Canon was composed before Jerome corrected the Latin translations of the gospel with reference to the old Greek manuscripts.

St Albert: To the apostles he joins certain martyrs of whose faith and of the motive of whose martyrdom there is perfect certainty. He mentions the outstanding martyrs whom the Roman Church had and still has in her bosom.

St Augustine: We do not commemorate the martyrs in the same way, as we do others who now rest in peace, as that we should also pray for them, but rather that they should pray for us, that we may follow their footsteps. For they have actually attained that fullness of love, than which, our Lord has told us, there cannot be a greater.

St Robert Bellarmine: It is not in the same way that we look for mercy from God through Christ's merits and intercessions and through the saints'. For we ask God for mercy directly through Christ, for he is our only direct mediator with God. But we ask that the merits and prayers of the saints may bring us God's mercy through the mediation of Christ; for they too, when they pray for us, pray through Christ.

St Antoninus: The Mass benefits the blessed when it is offered in their honour, by increasing their accidental glory. For they rejoice about every good thing which they see done in praise of God, and even more when it has some relation to themselves. They rejoice to see God being honoured in them and on their account.

ROMAN CANON: HANC IGITUR

We therefore beseech thee, O Lord, favourably to accept this offering of our slavery and that of all thy family, and to dispose our days in peace; and bid us be delivered from eternal damnation and be numbered among the company of thine elect. Through Christ our Lord. Amen.

Dom Guéranger: The priest, extending his hands over the oblation, prays anew. This gesture comes to us from the old Law. When a victim was presented in the temple, it was by means of this rite set apart for ever from all profane use, and devoted to the service and honour of God alone. So now, holy Church after having already, at the Offertory, removed the bread and wine from all profane use, and having offered them to God, does so now once again, and yet more earnestly, seeing that the moment of consecration is close at hand.

St Robert Bellarmine: Luther objects to this prayer, saying 'Here it offers bread and wine that the faithful may be freed from eternal damnation; so great a power do they attribute to bread and wine, while the passion and death of the Son of God is of no importance for their redemption.' But these are calumnies, not arguments. The priest is praying that God may accept the offering of bread and wine as the matter of the future sacrifice, that he might bless and sanctify it. He adds the three petitions mentioned, and prays that they should be answered, not through the offering of bread and wine, but *through Christ our Lord*.

Blessed Isaac of Stella: Three acts are seen in the sacred canon, carried out as it were on three altars, and being as it were three sacrifices. And perhaps this is the pattern that was shown to Moses on the mount, when he set up the shadow of the things to come, that is, the tabernacle in the desert. For in the forecourt there was a brazen altar, on which animals were sacrificed, within, a golden altar, called the altar of incense, on which incense and sweet-smelling spices were burned; and in the innermost part, in the holy of holies, a propitiatory was placed. All things being now ready for the first action, the visible priest now offers the visible sacrifices, which are *of the earth, earthly*, upon this visible and material altar, consecrated with visible oil. And all these things are done as it were, outside, for both what is done and how it is done are seen, therefore they pertain to the slave, *who abideth not in the house for ever*.

St Albert: Just as a victory does not belong to the king alone, but to all who helped him in any way to achieve the victory, so the oblation belongs not only to the priest but to all who in the service of God's house contribute something to its accomplishment. So the porter keeps the temple clean in which the oblation is to be made; the candle-bearer drives out darkness visible and invisible;

the exorcist excludes diabolic forces; the acolyte reveals the truth of the faith; the subdeacon brings the matter which is to be the sacrifice immolated in the sacrament; the deacon lays out the oblation and the corporal and the palls upon the altar; the priest perfects the oblation. *And all thy family* refers to the laymen, who are part of the sacrifice of the altar by their desires. Thus the whole army of the Church is a part of the oblation.

Blessed Isaac: Rightly does he call bread and wine an *offering of our slavery*, for man, whose nature was drawn from the earth, was by grace set as lord over the earth, but condemned by justice to go within the earth for his sin. And since bread and wine are chief among the victuals without which human life is not maintained, with them our bodily life is fittingly offered to God. For what can the servant do who desires to be reconciled with his Lord, but of his poverty to offer all his nourishment, and thus sacrifice his whole life? So in this first action, when in bread and wine he offers all his nourishment, he puts to death all that lives in an animal way within him; for he who withdraws nourishment, destroys life.

St Bede: Blessed Gregory added three perfect phrases to the celebration of Mass: *Mayst thou dispose our days in peace; and bid us to be delivered from eternal damnation, and to be numbered among the company of thine elect.*

Dom Guéranger: They were added when Rome was being besieged by the Lombards, and the city was in the utmost peril. Holy Church has judged it expedient to continue this petition for peace to the present day, mindful not to retrench from her text words given to so holy a pope by the Holy Ghost himself.

St Albert: He speaks of the elect whose names are written in the book of life, where they are written not because of present justice but by the grace of God's final choice. This was prefigured in the book of Esdras, where those who could not find their genealogy were separated from the people of the Lord, for they were not written down in the number of the saints. He concludes, *through Christ our Lord*, but no one answers *Amen,* as in the conclusion of the earlier silent prayers: unless it be the angels.

ROMAN CANON: QUAM OBLATIONEM

Which oblation, we beseech thee, O God, deign to make wholly ✠ *blessed,* ✠ *enrolled,* ✠ *established, reasonable and acceptable, that it may become for us the* ✠ *Body and* ✠ *Blood of thy most beloved Son, our Lord Jesus Christ.*

St Basil: Among the doctrines and teachings kept safe in the Church, some we have from written instruction, but others have been received by secret transmission, from the apostolic tradition. Yet all have the same importance for religion, and if one tried to banish the unwritten customs as unimportant, one would find that one had unwittingly harmed the gospel. Which saint passed on to us in writing the words of invocation, when the bread of the Eucharist and the cup of blessing are consecrated? Yet we do not limit ourselves to the words written in St Paul and in the gospels. Both before and after, other words are spoken of great importance for the Mystery, and these come from unwritten teaching.

St Thomas Aquinas: It is not inappropriate to ask God for something that we know with certainty he will do; thus, Christ asked that he might be glorified. Yet the priest does not seem to be asking here that the consecration may be effected, but rather that it may be fruitful for us, since he says, *That it may become for us the Body and Blood.* The words that precede also indicate this.

St Paschasius: For he says, *Deign to make this oblation wholly blessed*, that is, may we blessed by it; *enrolled*, that is, may it cause us to be written in heaven; *established*, that is, by it may we be reckoned as in the very heart of Christ; *rational*, that is, may it strip from us our brutal ways; and *acceptable*, that insofar as we are displeasing to ourselves, we may be made pleasing to the only-begotten Son.

St Albert: Five things are said to distinguish this oblation from the ancient ones. The ancient oblations were empty of grace, and so no blessing flowed from them. They were not *enrolled* for an everlasting memorial; they were invented by men, or ordained for God to keep men from idols. The old oblations were not *established*, but were proved on many accounts to be deficient. They were not *rational*, and so were overthrown, and they were never *acceptable* to the heart of God.

Durandus: Five crosses are made to indicate the time of the old Law, which was given in five books.

St Thomas Aquinas: Or, the second stage in Christ's passion was his being sold. Since he was sold to the priests, the scribes and the Pharisees, three crosses are made at the words, *blessed,* ✠ *enrolled,* ✠ *established*; or else this shows the price of the sale, thirty denarii. A double cross is added at the words, *ut nobis corpus et sanguis*, to denote Judas who made the sale and Christ who was sold.

Blessed Isaac: The servant has done all that he could in the first action, but it was not enough. He could kill, but he could not make alive. So he turns to the one who can do all things, and says, *Which oblation, we beseech thee, O Lord*, as if to say, 'I have done what I could; make good what I cannot do.' And not doubting in his faith, he begins the second action, saying, *Who the day before he suffered*, and those other words of power.

THE TWOFOLD CONSECRATION

*Who the day before he
suffered, took bread into his
holy and venerable hands;
and with eyes lifted to thee,
O God, his almighty Father,
giving thanks to thee,
did* ✠ *bless, break, and give to his disciples, saying:
Take and eat ye all of this.*

FOR THIS IS MY BODY

Dom Guéranger: *The day before he suffered.* These words were added by Pope Alexander I, the sixth successor of St Peter. He did this to recall the Passion, because the sacrifice of the Mass is one and the same with the sacrifice of the Cross.

Amalarius: What our Lord did at that Table corresponds to the whole work of the Mass. For it is said, *he took bread*, which is done by the priest when he takes the oblation at the Offertory. He *gives thanks*, in the preface; he *blesses* at this very place; he *breaks* before the Communion.

St Thomas Aquinas: Since Christ compared himself to a grain of wheat, saying, *Unless the grain of wheat falling*

127

into the ground die, itself remaineth alone, the matter of this sacrament is wheaten bread.

St Alphonsus: If he had chosen some rare or costly food, the poor would have been deprived of this, of him. No, Jesus would come under the form of bread, which costs little and can be found everywhere, so that he would be most accessible to all.

St Paschasius: Put no salt or honey in it, as some wish to do, nor add or take away anything, but just as Christ has instituted it, so must you believe and understand it to be done.

St Albert: By the touch of his holy and divine hands, he conferred on the matter of the sacrament a power for all time to be transubstantiated into the body of Christ, just as by contact with his all-pure flesh he gave to water the power of regeneration. Hence it is said in the Canticle of Canticles, *his hands are rounded gold, full of hyacinths*.

St Thomas Aquinas: As John says, many things were done by our Lord which the evangelists did not write. One of these is that he raised his eyes to heaven at the Supper. Yet the Church knows this by apostolic tradition.

St Leonard: The sacrifice was instituted by our Redeemer principally in recognition of the beneficence of God, and as *thanks* to him; and therefore it bears as its most special and worthy name, the *Eucharist*, which signifies 'an offering of thanks'.

St Thomas Aquinas: The third stage of the passion was its being prefigured by Christ at the Last Supper. To show this, one sign of the cross is made at the consecration of the Body and another at the consecration of the Blood, when the word *bless* is spoken.

St Augustine: What else is the sign of Christ but the cross of Christ? For unless that sign be applied, whether it be to the foreheads of believers, or to the very water out of which they are regenerated, or to the oil with which they receive the anointing chrism, or to the sacrifice that nourishes them, none of them is properly administered.

St Ambrose: Before, the priest gave praise to God, and prayed for the people, for kings and for others. But when he comes to consecrate the adorable sacrament, the priest no longer uses his own words, but the words of Christ. Before the words of the sacrament, it is bread in common use; after consecration it becomes from bread Christ's flesh.

St Vincent Ferrer: When the words of consecration are said, Christ truly descends into the host and the whole substance of the bread is converted into the true flesh of Christ. He is as truly in the host when the words of consecration have been completed as he was in the womb of the Virgin Mary when she had spoken those words, *Behold, the handmaid of the Lord: be it done to me according to thy word.*

St Peter Damian: The bread and wine are changed into the flesh and blood by that word of power by which the Word became flesh and dwelled among us; by which he spoke and they were made; by which the woman was converted into a statue;[19] by which the rod was changed

---

19. Lot's wife.

into a serpent; by which the springs became blood and water changed into wine. For if the word of Elias could bring down fire from heaven, will the word of Christ be unable to change bread into flesh?

St Paschasius: The words of Christ, since they are divine, are efficacious, and can produce nothing other than what they command. For they are eternal. *Heaven and earth shall pass, but my words shall not pass.*

Blessed Isaac: Above all human understanding, therefore, by divine power and by human care, from the old food of the old man comes the new food of the new man.

St Robert Bellarmine: Christ spoke these words not only to consecrate, but also to teach the apostles the rite of consecration. Therefore he had to speak aloud, to be heard by the apostles. Bishops do the same to this day, when they ordain priests at Mass; they pronounce the words of consecration aloud, so that all the new priests may hear them.

Dom Guéranger: The moment that these words of consecration are uttered, the priest on bended knees adores the sacred host. The bread has gone, there remain now but the species, the appearances; it has yielded its place to the Lord. From this moment, each time that the priest touches the host, he will genuflect both before and after doing so; before, because he is going to touch the Lord, and after, in order to pay him homage. Besides this, he will not disjoin the thumb and index finger of each hand, until the ablution, because these fingers are sacred, and have alone the honour of touching the Lord.

St Thomas Aquinas: This is done so that if a particle of the host adheres to his fingers, it may not be lost.

Durandus: Again, the fingers that touched the body of Christ are conjoined to show that the faithful, who touch it also by faith and devotion, must be joined together by charity.

St Antoninus: When the meal was prepared for him, all Isaac's senses were deceived except for the sense of hearing. For his sight, which had grown dim, did not perceive Jacob in front of him; his power of smell perceived the fragrance of Esau's garments, not of Jacob's; his taste supposed that he was eating food prepared by Esau, not by Jacob; his sense of touch was deceived, for *the hands* were *the hands of Esau*, because of the goats' skins with which the arms were covered. Only hearing was not misled, for he said, *The voice is the voice of Jacob*. So in this sacrament, taste, smell, sight and touch perceive the accidents of bread just as they were; but hearing is not deceived, when it hears, *This is my body*.

THE TWOFOLD CONSECRATION

In like manner, after he had supped, taking also this precious chalice into his holy and adorable hands, and giving thanks to thee, he ✝ blessed and gave to his disciples saying:
Take and drink ye all of this.

FOR THIS IS THE CHALICE
OF MY BLOOD OF THE NEW AND
ETERNAL TESTAMENT,
THE MYSTERY OF FAITH:
WHICH SHALL BE SHED FOR YOU
AND FOR MANY
UNTO THE REMISSION OF SINS.

As often as ye shall do these things, ye shall do them in remembrance of me.

St Thomas Aquinas: Just as our Lord compared himself to a grain of wheat, so also he compared himself to a vine: *I am the true vine.* Therefore only wine from the vine, as only wheaten bread, is the proper matter of this sacrament.

St Albert: He *supped* both of the figurative lamb, and of his own body. He took the *outstanding chalice*, that is, the one that stands before all others. For of the chalice of the Old Testament he said, *I will not drink from henceforth of this fruit of the vine*. But of this one he says, 'Until it is fulfilled in the kingdom of God', that is, made strong in the might of the Church. And this precious chalice he daily drinks and imbibes in his members. *And again he gave thanks*, for the redemption of the human race by his blood.

St Paschasius: For as in his members he himself suffers and hungers and thirsts and is clothed and is harboured, so he *drinks it new in the Kingdom of the Father*, that is, in the Church, as often as his own eat or drink him worthily.

Remigius: He says, *He took this chalice*, because the Catholic priest sacrifices no other chalice than that which our Lord passed on to the apostles. For just as the divinity of the Word of God is one and fills the whole world, so although this body is consecrated in many places and on countless days, yet there are not many bodies of Christ, nor many chalices, but one body and one blood, which he took in the womb of the Virgin, and gave to the apostles.

St Thomas Aquinas: It is objected that none of the evangelists record that Christ spoke all these words. In reply, it must be said that the evangelists' intention was not to pass on the forms of the sacraments, which had to be kept hidden in the primitive Church, but to tell the story of Christ. Yet almost all these words can be found in diverse places in Scripture. For St Luke and

St Paul have *This is the chalice,* and St Matthew has *This is my blood of the new Covenant, which will be poured out for many for the remission of sins.* The words *eternal* and *mystery of faith,* come from a tradition going back to our Lord, which came to the Church through the apostles: as St Paul says, *I received of the Lord that which also I delivered unto you.*

Durandus: For who would have been so bold as to have interposed these words by his own initiative?

St Vincent Ferrer: Of this sacramental form Paul said to Timothy, *Hold the form of sound words, which thou hast heard of me in faith, and in the love which is in Christ Jesus.*

St Thomas Aquinas: A testament sets an inheritance in order. Now God ordained that the heavenly inheritance should be given to men by the power of the blood of Jesus Christ. This blood was first shown to men in figures, under the old testament; but then it was shown in all truth, under the *new testament.* This testament is *eternal* because it was ordained by God from eternity, and because it gives access to an eternal inheritance; and because Christ whose blood ratified the testament is an eternal person. It is called the *mystery of faith* because only faith can hold that the blood of Christ is truly in this sacrament. Again, the passion of Christ justifies men through faith.

Amalarius: The word *Mysterium* comes from Greek, and means a secret. Since the faith lies hid in the hearts of God's chosen, it is called 'the secret of faith'.

Dom Guéranger: It is this mystery which specially

and above all others proves our faith: for, according to the word of St Peter, our faith must needs be proved. So St Paul, writing to Timothy, tells him, on the subject of the Eucharist that deacons should be pure and holy, *holding the mystery of faith in a pure conscience.*

St Thomas Aquinas: The blood of Christ benefits not only the Jews, who were chosen to see the blood of the Old Testament, but also the Gentiles. Nor does it benefit only the priests who confect this sacrament or those who receive it, but also those for whom it is offered. Therefore he says, *for you*, the Jews, *and for many*, that is, the Gentiles; or *for you* who receive it, *and for many*, for whom it is offered.

St Albert: It is asked, 'Why did he not say "for all"?' Some reply that while the blood of Christ truly suffices for all, yet since not all but many are saved, he said 'for many' rather than 'for all'. And this reply is good and Catholic. But one who considers our Lord's words more closely may see that 'for many' signifies more than 'for all'. For 'many' signifies a multitude, which may increase indefinitely. But 'all' would indicate some complete group; and this would not express the fact that the Blood would also suffice for something greater than this total group of people.

St Francis de Sales: 'Do this in my remembrance': it is as if he should say, 'Remember what I endured for your salvation, and practise this same mystery for yourselves and for those dear to you.'

St Robert Bellarmine: The words of Christ, *Do this*, were spoken only to the apostles, who by this command were ordained the first priests of the new Testament. These words do not mean simply 'Eat and drink', which pertains to all Christians, but also, 'Consecrate, receive, and distribute to others, as you have seen me do.'

Remigius: Therefore by the power and the words of Christ, this bread and chalice have been consecrated from the beginning, and are consecrated now, and will always be consecrated.

Dom Guéranger: Though this is to be the work of antichrist: he will take every possible means to prevent the celebration of the holy sacrifice of the Mass.

St Robert Bellarmine: St Paul explains *in remembrance of me*, in these words, *you shall show the death of the Lord until he come*. We are commanded, then, to receive the Eucharist in remembrance of our Lord's passion and death.

St Antoninus: The psalmist says, *The voice of the Lord in magnificence*. And this is that voice, when the priest says, *For this is my Body*, and over the mingled chalice, *For this is the chalice of my Blood* and what follows. What magnificence is in that voice, that bread and wine should be changed by it into the body and blood of Christ!

ELEVATION

St Leonard: Behold the Sun of holy Church, that scatters the clouds and renders heaven again serene! Behold the heavenly Rainbow, pacifying the storms of divine justice!

St Vincent Ferrer: Behold, the everlasting oblation! Of such power it is, that in the whole world no other sacrifice remains but this.

Alcuin: The same is Victor and Victim, and Victor because Victim. The same is Sacrificer and Sacrifice, and Sacrificer because Sacrifice.

St Vincent Ferrer: The whole life and passion of Christ is expressed in the Mass. So when the priest raises the sacred host and chalice, he represents how Christ was raised high upon the Cross. All must humble themselves and bend the knee when the body of Christ is raised up, for the true Christ who is in heaven is in the host. Do not copy those wretched men who neither bend their knees nor bare their heads. For the prophet David says to the priests, *Exalt the Lord your God*, and then to everyone, *And adore his footstool*, that is, the host.

St Ambrose: By the *footstool* is understood the earth, and by the earth is understood the flesh of Christ, which we today adore in the mysteries and which the apostles adored in the Lord Jesus.

St Francis de Sales: At the elevation of the most holy Sacrament, we must strive to adore him with all our heart, then to offer him to God the Father for the remission of our sins and those of all the world, then to offer to him ourselves and all the Church and all our relations and friends.

Durandus: For the elevation is done that all present may see and ask for whatever will profit unto salvation, according to the words, *And I, if I be lifted up from the earth, will draw all things to myself.*

ROMAN CANON: UNDE ET MEMORES

Wherefore, O Lord, we thy servants, as also thy holy people, calling to mind the blessed passion of the same Christ thy Son, our Lord, and also his resurrection from hell and glorious ascension into heaven, offer unto thy most excellent majesty, of thy presents and gifts, a pure ✠ host, a holy ✠ host, a spotless ✠ host, the holy bread ✠ of eternal life, and the chalice ✠ of everlasting salvation.

Amalarius: He himself said, *As often as ye shall do these things, ye shall do them in remembrance of me.* That is, 'as often as you have blessed this Bread and Chalice, remember my birth as man, my passion and my resurrection.'

St Thomas Aquinas: By saying, *Wherefore,* the priest is excusing his presumption, indicating that he has acted out of obedience to the command of Christ.

St Leonard: Observe that in Mass, there is made not a simple commemoration or representation of the passion and death of our redeemer; there is performed in a certain true sense, the selfsame most holy act which was performed on Calvary.

Blessed Columba Marmion: Although the Eucharist recalls directly and principally the passion of Jesus, it does not exclude the remembrance of the glorious mysteries that are very closed linked to the passion, of which they are, in a sense, the crown.

St Albert: Why is mention made of his resurrection and ascension, when this sacrament is a commemoration of the passion? The resurrection is named because the sacrament of the Eucharist is able to place within us the seed of immortality. The ascension is named because this sacrament leads us to the fatherland, and is a sign of the food prepared for us in heaven. Yet no mention is made of his return in judgement: for the return of Christ will cause fear and terror, and this sacrament is the gift of charity and of peace.

St Robert Bellarmine: This offering that follows the consecration is the whole Church bearing witness that she consents to the offering made by Christ, and offers it along with him.

Dom Guéranger: She steps forward as the bride in the presence of the glorious Trinity, and says, 'I am endowed with thine own riches, I possess him as mine own, who has performed all this that I am now calling to mind; he is mine, for thou hast given him to me. Behold, I offer him unto thee, and this my offering is worthy of thee.'

St Leonard: With this sacrifice, each one of the faithful nobly honours God, confessing both his own nothingness and the supreme dominion which God has over him; and so David calls it *the sacrifice of justice.*

Blessed Isaac: From the divine presents and gifts, he offers the heavenly sacrifice of flesh and blood from heaven, not speaking hesitantly as before, nor calling it *the sacrifice of our slavery*, but with joy and gladness offering it *to thy most excellent majesty.* The first offering separated him from the world; the second joins him to Christ. The first put him to death; the second brings him to life.

St Peter Damian: *Of thy presents*, that is, from the produce of crops, which refers to the bread consecrated into the flesh. And *of thy gifts*, that is, from the produce of trees, which refers to the wine consecrated into the blood. *A pure ✠ host, a holy ✠ host, a spotless ✠ host* that is, the Eucharist is free from every possible fault, whether original, venial or criminal.

St Robert Bellarmine: Most rightly may Christ be called a present and gift from God. And this sacrament, and this sacrifice, what is it but a most true present and gift from God?

St Albert: Or, He says *presents* to refer to what is of grace, and *gifts* to refer to the natural things that God gives in creation. He says *a pure host, a holy host, a spotless host* to refer not to the true body of Christ, but to the mystical body, which he prays may be incorporated into the true body and so offered to God. This has the impurity of original sin, and the uncleanness of actual sin, and the contagious stain of venial sin, and so he asks that against these three things, the mystical body must be purified, sanctified and made spotless by the true body of Christ. And at these words, the priest makes three crosses, to show that the fullness of blessing comes from the giver of holiness into the mystical body, of which the true body is here as a sign.

St Peter Damian: Or, since he has said that he is mindful of our Lord's passion, he straightway commemorates the sharpness of that passion, bringing to mind by five crosses the five wounds.

St Thomas Aquinas: After the consecration, the priest does not make the sign of the cross in order to bless or consecrate, but simply to recall the power of the cross, and the manner in which Christ died.

St Albert: The priest, as the giver of sanctity, recites all the prayers with his arms cruciform, to show the people an image of Christ on the Cross, fulfilling the figure of Moses who also prayed in this way, and to show that he is ready to receive all into the embrace of charity, as it is said, *I have spread forth my hands all the day to an unbelieving people*. Yet this prayer he says with his hands raised on high and stretched forth more than at other times, to show his intention that the sacrifice may be raised to heaven, as if to say, 'The raising of my hands is as the evening sacrifice, which Christ raised up to heaven in the evening of the world.'

St Peter Damian: The *holy bread*, that is, able to make men holy and to give *eternal life*. This is said in reference to the glory of the body. And *the chalice of everlasting salvation*, which is said in reference to the glory of the soul.

ROMAN CANON: SUPRA QUAE PROPITIO

Upon which vouchsafe to look with a propitious and serene countenance, and to accept them, as thou wert graciously pleased to accept the gifts of thy righteous child Abel, and the sacrifice of our patriarch Abraham and that which thy high priest Melchisedech offered to thee, a holy sacrifice, a spotless host.

St Thomas Aquinas: Now the priest prays that the sacrifice that has been performed may be accepted by God.

St Robert Bellarmine: For although the consecrated offering is always pleasing to God both in itself and because of Christ who principally offers it, yet in respect of the minister or the people present who offer with him, it may not be pleasing. Therefore we pray that God may look kindly upon this offering, inasmuch as it is offered by us.

St Albert: He says, *Vouchsafe to look*, that is, with the eye of love. For where love is, there is the eye.

St Peter Damian: Not that God's countenance can

ever change; but he is said to enlighten us with a bright countenance when he shows his mercy to us and makes it clearly known.

St Albert: He enumerates three figures of this sacrament, each of which reveals something of its meaning. Abel's sacrifice prefigures the death of Christ; Abraham's prefigures Christ's dignity as the only-begotten; Melchisedech's prefigures the rite and the truth of this sacrament. He says, *as thou wert pleased*, not to indicate equality, since our sacrifice is far more acceptable than theirs, but to denote the likeness of a reality to what prefigured it.

St Robert Bellarmine: Before the incarnation, since Christ was not yet literally a priest, he could not offer sacrifice directly. Yet so that he might be called a priest even at that time, and might be high priest from the beginning of the world to its end, he offered sacrifice in the way that was then possible, that is, through types and figures. For as all the ancient sacrifices prefigured the sacrifice of the Cross, and in all those victims, he, the immaculate lamb, was slain in type, and so he is called *the Lamb slain from the foundation of the world*, so also all those priests were types of Christ, and he offered sacrifice in their sacrifices.

St Albert: He says, *thy child Abel*, a child, that is, by his obedience and purity, though not in his thinking. He speaks of *Abraham*, 'who offered to thee his only-begotten, yet slew a ram in his place, for in this sacrifice the deity of thy only begotten is offered to thee, though not slain even in symbol, but his humanity, prefigured by the ram, is mystically immolated.'

St Jerome: Turn to the book of Genesis, and you will find Melchisedech, king of Salem, who even then offered bread and wine as a type of Christ, inaugurating the Christian mystery of the body and blood of our Saviour.

St Augustine: Then first appeared the sacrifice that is now offered to God by Christians throughout the whole earth. And thus is fulfilled what was said in prophecy to Christ, when he was yet to come in the flesh: *Thou art a priest forever according to the order of Melchisedech.*

St Albert: Note that these three figurative sacrifices were all offered under the law of nature, and were accepted because of the faith of the forefathers. But the sacrifices of the law of Moses were not accepted, but rather tolerated by God for a time, that they might at least be offered to him, rather than to idols.

St Robert Bellarmine: In his life of Pope Leo I,[20] the author of the *Liber Pontificalis* notes that the words *a holy sacrifice, a spotless host* were added to the Canon by this pope. This is a clear proof that the Canon is more ancient than Leo, and was already by his time long held in the greatest veneration: for why else would a historian have noted so carefully that he had added to it a particular word or phrase?

---

20. He died in 461 AD.

Roman Canon:

Supplices te Rogamus

We most humbly beseech thee, almighty God, command these things to be carried by the hands of thy holy angel to thine altar on high, in the sight of thy divine majesty; that as many of us, as by participation at this altar shall receive the most sacred ✠ body and ✠ blood of thy Son, may be filled with all heavenly ✠ blessing and grace. Through the same Christ our Lord. Amen.

St Thomas Aquinas: Next the priest requests that this sacrifice and sacrament may accomplish its effect, first for those who receive it, at the words, *We most humbly beseech thee*, then for the dead, who may no longer receive it, at the words, *Be mindful, also.*

St Leonard: For as there is renewed in the Mass the offering which Jesus has already made on the cross to the eternal Father for the sins of the whole world, that same divine blood which was once paid as the general ransom of the human race comes to be applied to each of us individually, by being offered at Mass for the sins of him who celebrates and of all those who assist.

St Albert: The priest speaks this prayer bowed low before the altar, to show by his body the mind's humility, remembering how it was said, *The prayer of him that humbleth himself shall pierce the clouds.*

Blessed Isaac: He seeks something still higher than before, something which he cannot reach until he shall be united to God in heaven through the Body, and joined through the humanity to the divinity. Therefore he proceeds to the third action. But since he cannot yet ascend to the altar on high where the perpetual high priest ministers before the face of the Father, the visible priest bows low before the visible altar and kisses it.

St Peter Damian: The words, *command these things*, and what follows, are words of such depth that the mind of man is scarcely able to penetrate their meaning.

St Robert Bellarmine: These words must not be understood so unintelligently, as if some visible and bodily altar were set up in heaven; nevertheless, that there is some spiritual altar in heaven, as also a tabernacle, a throne, incense, trumpets, crowns, palms, and other such things, no one can deny who does not wish to deny the Scriptures. Either that heavenly altar is Christ, through whom our prayers and offerings ascend to God, or else there is said to be an altar in heaven because the sacrifices offered on earth are received in heaven.

Blessed Columba Marmion: The Church wishes to point out that there is but one sacrifice: the immolation which is accomplished mystically on earth is one with the offering that Christ our high priest makes of himself in the bosom of the Father, to whom he offers for us the satisfactions of his Passion.

Amalarius: How great and wonderful is the faith of holy Church, whose eyes see that which is not present to mortals! She sees what she must believe, though she does not yet see it as it is. She believes this sacrifice is carried by the hands of angels into the presence of our Lord, which she knows to be taken between the teeth of men.

St Thomas Aquinas: He is not asking either that the sacramental appearances should be brought to heaven, or that the true body of Christ should be, for this never ceases to be there. Rather, he is asking that this may be done for the mystical body of Christ, symbolised by this sacrament; that is, that the angel present at the divine mysteries may bring the prayers of the priest and the people to God, according to that word, *The smoke of the incense of the prayers of the saints ascended up before God from the hand of the angel.* Or else, by *the angel*, we may understand Christ himself, who is the *angel of great counsel*, and who joins his mystical body to God the Father and to the Church triumphant.

St Augustine: If there is a spiritual sacrifice, an eternal sacrifice of praise, there must also be an eternal priest and an eternal altar, which is nothing else but the souls of the just, finally at peace.

St Thomas Aquinas: The *altar of God on high* is either the Church triumphant, to which we ask to be brought, or God himself, in whom we desire to have a share.

St Albert: *The divine majesty* looked forth from the mercy seat, within the holy of holies, towards the altar of incense. That altar, made of bright gold, was the blessed shining divinity of the Son of man. Thus the sacrifice is borne to the *sublime altar of God* when all within this sacrifice cleave to the deity of Christ present before the Father's majesty.

Blessed Isaac: He seeks to be united to the body of Christ in heaven, so that just as we take what seems like bread and wine from the first altar, and the true body and blood from the second, he may also by the power of the sacrament share beyond the veil in heaven in the *blessing* once promised to Abraham and the *grace* bestowed on Mary, being united to the supreme Head through the spirit. For *the head of Christ is God*. So the first sacrifice, as it were in the forecourt, pertained to animal life; the second, inside the temple, pertained to the judgement of reason; the third beyond the veil and in heaven is of faith. For the judgement of reason is set above animal life, and faith is set above the judgement of reason, and above faith is vision.

St Robert Bellarmine: These words, *As many of us as by participation*, and what follows, refer both to any communicants present at the Mass and to those who receive communion elsewhere. For since we are one body, we pray not only for those present but also for those absent from us. In like manner, anyone may recite the Lord's prayer when alone in his chamber, even though it is phrased as if it were to be said only by many people together.

St Albert: The priest kisses the altar, to show his fellowship with all who offer the sacrifice of the altar.

St Thomas Aquinas: The altar symbolizes Christ himself, of whom the Apostle says, *By him we offer the sacrifice of praise to God*.

St Albert: When he says *the body*, he makes a cross upon it, to show that the fullness of blessing comes from the first giver of holiness into the mystical body. And when he says *the blood*, he makes another cross to show that grace also comes into the same mystical body. And when he says *all heavenly blessing*, the priest makes a cross upon himself, to show that the same grace flows from God to him, a weak man, who is offering both for himself and for the people.

St Thomas Aquinas: By these three crosses, he represents the stretching forth of the body upon the cross, and the shedding of the blood, and the fruit of the passion.

Blessed Columbia Marmion: Each Mass truly contains all the fruits of the sacrifice of the Cross. But, if we wish to avail ourselves of them, we must enter into the dispositions of the heart of Jesus, when he went to offer himself on Calvary: *Let this mind be in you, which was also in Christ Jesus*.

St Leonard: Take my advice, and in every Mass ask God to make you a great saint. Does this seem too much? It is not too much. Is it not our good Master who declares in the holy gospel that for a cup of cold water given out of love for him, he will, in return, give paradise? How then while offering to God the blood of his most blessed Son, should he not give you a hundred heavens, were there so many?

ROMAN CANON: MEMENTO OF THE DEAD

Be mindful, also, O Lord, of thy servants and handmaids who are gone before us with the sign of faith and sleep in the sleep of peace, N. and N. To these, O Lord, and to all that rest in Christ, grant, we beseech thee, a place of refreshment, light and peace. Through the same Christ our Lord. Amen.

St Augustine: It is not to be doubted but that the dead can be helped by the prayers of holy Church, and the eucharistic sacrifice, and alms distributed for the repose of their spirits, so that God may deal with them more mercifully than their sins have deserved. The whole Church, I mean, observes this tradition received from the fathers, that prayers should be offered for those who have died in the communion of the body and blood of Christ, whenever their names are mentioned in the sacrifice in the usual place. There can be no doubt that all these things are of value to the departed, but only to those of them as lived in such a way before they died as would enable them to profit from these things after death.

St Isidore: Since this is done throughout the world, we believe that it is a tradition received from the apostles.

St Cyril of Jerusalem: Surely, if, when a king had banished certain people who had given him offence, their connexions should weave a crown and offer it to him on behalf of those under his vengeance, would he not grant a respite to their punishments? And when we offer to him our supplications for those who have fallen asleep, though we weave no crown, yet we offer up Christ, sacrificed for our sins, propitiating our merciful God both for them and for ourselves.

St Gregory: For this reason, the souls of the dead sometimes beg to have Masses offered for them.

St Albert: For this sacrifice freed the fathers who were held in Limbo, when it was offered on the altar of the Cross.

Dom Guéranger: What does the Church understand by *the sign of faith*? It is the sign of baptism, and of confirmation, which latter makes the perfect Christian.

St Albert: They preceded us by dying *with the sign of faith*, that is, by receiving the sacrament of faith with reverence and adoration. *They sleep in the sleep of peace*: indeed, the death of the devout is a sleep, since in one who sleeps the hidden life is present more than in one who is awake, whereas their public life is bound. So it is with those who have died with the sign of faith; the life of grace is more active in them than in the living, but the public life that works through the body is bound until the resurrection of the flesh.

St Robert Bellarmine: Luther objects that this prayer fights against itself and destroys itself. For we pray for those who *sleep in the sleep of peace*, and who *rest in Christ*, and yet we ask for them *a place of refreshment, light and peace*. But if they sleep and rest, why do we seek refreshment for them? And if they have peace, why do we desire peace for them? I reply: they have a certain peace and rest, since they are sure of the reward of eternal joy, and free from the strife with temptations and concupiscence, and from every evil deed. But they do not have the peace and rest that would come from an end to their torments, and an end to their desire for the vision of God. This prayer, in fact, could not be more aptly composed if it is to refer only to those who are in purgatory. For those in hell have no peace or rest; those in the Kingdom possess all peace and rest; only those who suffer in purgatory so rest in the sleep of peace that they still need peace and refreshment.

Dom Guéranger: What is purgatory? It is a place in which souls stand in need of refreshment, for those piercing flames are keenly felt. Moreover, it is a place where there is no light, since holy Church craves for these poor souls, *a place of light*. Furthermore, it is a place where pleasant peace reigns not, the soul striving towards God whom it may not reach. Whenever we pray for the dead, the succour that reaches them by our means, is always in the form of refreshment, light, and peace.

St Albert: They await the end of their purgation with sure hope in peace of heart. The souls in purgatory are not afflicted by the demons, but rather are purged through themselves, as gold is purged and shines in the fire. The souls that leave the body tend downwards more or less according to the weight of the venial sins that they bear with them, like heavy objects of various weight. And so in the prophet Zechariah, *wickedness* is said to sit upon *a talent of lead*.

St Leonard: One Mass alone, considered in itself and according to its own intrinsic value, is sufficient to empty purgatory of all the souls in process of purification and place them in paradise. For this divine sacrifice not only avails for the souls of the dead as a propitiation, but also as a great act of supplication, conformably to the practice of the Church, which not only offers Mass for the souls that are being purified, but also prays during the sacrifice for their liberation.

St Albert: With this faith, the Catholic Church offers for all the departed. For she will presume of anyone that he is in a place of purgation, since she cannot be sure of the final impenitence of anyone, God alone knowing the hearts of those who die. And the Church devoutly believes that many even after they have lost the power of speech yet sigh for their sins with saving sorrow.

ROMAN CANON: NOBIS QUOQUE PECCATORIBUS

*And to us sinners: thy
servants, trusting in the
multitude of thy mercies, vouchsafe to grant some part
and fellowship with thy holy apostles and martyrs:
with John, Stephen, Matthias, Barnabas, Ignatius,
Alexander, Marcellinus, Peter, Felicity, Perpetua,
Agatha, Lucy, Agnes, Cecily, Anastasia, and with
all thy saints: into whose company we beseech thee
to admit us, not considering our merit, but freely
pardoning our offences. Through Christ our Lord.*

St Albert: He says, *And to us sinners*, who intercede for
others, when we ourselves have greater need of others'
prayers. Therefore the priest at this moment raises his
voice a little and strikes his breast. The striking denotes
the work of satisfying for sin, since a blow brings pain.
The audible speech denotes the act of confession.

St Peter Damian: The priest makes allusion to what
was done during the Passion, not only by the mark of

the cross, but also by the tone of his voice. Therefore he breaks the silence here, striking his breast and raising his voice a little, to show the contrition and confession of the good thief. Or perhaps by raising his voice and striking his breast, he recalls that *The centurion and they that were with him watching Jesus, having seen the things that were done, were sore afraid, saying: Indeed this was the Son of God. And all the multitude of them that were come together returned striking their breasts.*

Amalarius: Had heathendom not been destined to be steeped in the mystery of the Water and the Blood, the centurion would not have changed as he did. For he felt such great compunction that he cried out plainly in the greatness of his emotion, *Indeed this was the Son of God.* And the priest expresses this change by changing his voice, saying aloud, *And to us sinners.*

Durandus: In the commemoration of the saints before the body of Christ is consecrated, their prayers were requested; now that the body of Christ has been consecrated, the company of the saints is sought. For before the body of Christ, which is the Church universal, has been consecrated, that is, before the Kingdom comes, we who are on pilgrimage require prayers. But when the body of Christ is once consecrated, that is, when the Kingdom has come, we shall enjoy the company of the saints in our homeland

St Albert: The *fellowship* of the saints in beatitude means that the goods of each become common to all.

St Robert Bellarmine: Stephen is mentioned before the Apostle Matthias because the Church follows here the order of martyrdom, not of dignity. For Stephen suffered before Matthias. As for why Matthias is not mentioned with the other apostles before the consecration, I think there are two reasons. The first is that one of the twelve apostles might be mentioned in this list, that it might be truly said, *With thy holy apostles and martyrs.* The other is because Matthias was not an apostle before the passion of our Lord.

St Peter Damian: He does not recompense us as our *merits* deserve, for he punishes less and rewards more than mere justice would require.

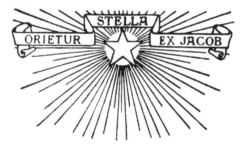

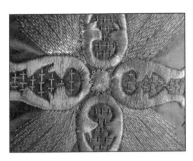

ROMAN CANON: PER QUEM HAEC OMNIA

Through whom, O Lord, thou dost always create, ✠
sanctify, ✠ *quicken,* ✠ *bless, and give us these good*
things. Through ✠ *him, and with* ✠ *him, and in* ✠
him, is to thee, God, ✠ *the Father almighty, in the*
unity of the ✠ *Holy Ghost, all honour and glory:*

For ever and ever.

St Robert Bellarmine: These words bring the Canon
to a most fitting end, since they briefly enumerate all
God's blessings in this sacrament, beginning with the
first production of the matter with which it is confected.
It is first of all *created*, when the bread is created. It is
sanctified when it is dedicated at the offertory as that from
which the sacrament will come. It is *quickened* when the
mystery of life is wrought, and by the consecration it
is changed into the true body of the Lord, who is our
life. It is *blessed* when it obtains the effect for which all
blessings are given, that is, when it unites the members
with the Head by its sacramental power. It is *given*, when
we receive it so that we may draw life therefrom.

St Albert: The sign of the cross is made to show that the power of the cross accomplishes these things. But it is not made at the word *create*, for God does this without us, nor at the word, *give*, again to emphasise that God does this from sheer goodness.

St Peter Damian: *These things*, that is, the bread, wine and water.

St Antoninus: *Through him*, that is, through Christ our Lord, whence this sacrament takes its origin. It derives from him as a natural reality, and so the priest says *create*; it derives from him as a sacrament, and so he says, *sanctify*; it derives from him in its power, and so he says both *quicken*, for the effect of grace is to vivify the soul, and *bless*, for the sacrament also increases grace; and since Christ gave this sacrament to us to use, he says, *give*.

Durandus: The pall is removed from the chalice to denote that when Christ gave up the ghost, the veil of the temple was torn from top to bottom, and those things which had before been concealed were made known to us.

St Thomas Aquinas: Here is represented the threefold prayer that Christ offered upon the Cross: once, for his persecutors, when he said, *Father, forgive them*; once for deliverance from death, when he said, *My God, My God, why hast thou forsaken me?*; and once for his glorification, when he said, *Father, into thy hands I commend my spirit*. To represent this, the priest makes the threefold sign of the cross at the words, *sanctify, quicken, bless*. Then are represented the three hours during which he hung on the Cross, that is, from the sixth to the ninth hour. To symbolise this, the priest again makes a triple sign of the Cross, at the words, *Through him, with him, in him.*

Durandus: *In him*, that is, in his members.

St Peter Damian: To represent the division of our Lord's flesh from his soul as he died, the priest makes two crosses by the mouth of the chalice, saying, *to thee, God the Father almighty.* Or, the two crosses which he makes at the side of the chalice represent the two sacraments that flowed forth from our Lord's side, that is, the water of rebirth and the blood of redemption.

Amalarius: The priest makes two crosses with the host beside the chalice, to show that the one who has been taken down from the Cross was crucified for both peoples.

Dom Guéranger: This time the priest makes the sign of the cross between the chalice and his own breast. Why this difference? He is pronouncing these words: *to thee, God the Father almighty, in the unity of the Holy Ghost*; as neither the Father, nor the Holy Ghost have been immolated, it would be unbecoming, whilst naming them, to place the host over the blood which belongs to the Son alone.

St Peter Damian: In all, the sacrifice is marked seven times with the sign of the cross: twice with two crosses, twice with three crosses, and thrice with five crosses, or in all, five times five, or twenty five crosses. And this is a number that always remains when multiplied by itself, for five times five is twenty five, and twenty five times five is one hundred and twenty five, and one hundred and twenty five times five is six hundred and twenty five. And so this number always increases and returns and is ever present even if one should multiply it without end. Even so the sacrament of the Eucharist is ever the same sacrifice.

Durandus: The sacrifice is signed with the cross at seven different stages of the canon. This expresses the sevenfold grace of the Holy Ghost, which is necessary in this mystery.

St Thomas Aquinas: It can also be said that the consecration of this sacrament, and the acceptation of this sacrifice, and the benefit that it confers all derive from the power of Christ's Cross; and so whenever mention is made of any of these things, the priest makes the sign of the cross.

St Peter Damian: Because *Jesus crying with a loud voice yielded up the ghost*, the priest lifts his voice, saying *per omnia saecula saeculorum*. Because the women bewailed and lamented him, the choir answers *Amen*. And because *a great stone was rolled at the door of the tomb*, the deacon covers the chalice once more with the pall.

St Justin: And when the prayers and thanksgiving have been offered, all who are present second what is done, and say, *Amen*.

PATER NOSTER

Taught by saving precepts and following divine direction, we presume to say: Our Father . . .

Dom Guéranger: As in our own day, so in all past ages, our Lord's prayer has had a place in the course of the holy sacrifice, for we meet with it in every liturgy and in every canon of the Mass.

St Peter Damian: Blessed Gregory ordained that it should be said over the oblation itself.[21]

St Gregory: Indeed, it seemed to me very unsuitable that we should say over the oblation a prayer which a learned man had composed, and should not say the very prayer which our Redeemer composed, while his body and blood are before us. Now, among the Greeks, this prayer is said by all the people, but with us by the priest alone.

St Peter Damian: Jesus cried with a loud voice, *Father, into thy hands I commend my spirit*, and so the priest lifts up his voice and says, *Our Father, who art in heaven.*

Durandus: In the law, the high priest returned to the people and washed his garments, but remained unclean until

---

21. That is, not after the consecrated species had been taken from the altar in preparation for the communion of the faithful, as had previously been done.

evening. Likewise Christ, who has entered into the holy of holies returns to the Church by showing compassion and bringing aid, and he washes his garments, that is, he purifies the saints, and yet some stains cling to these members of his until the end of the world. So also the priest seems to come back out to the people when he begins once again to pray in a clear voice, and with prayers as with water he washes and purifies his garments, that is, the people; and yet he is judged unclean, since until death, something remains in every man still in need of purgation.

St Francis de Sales: When the priest says the *Pater*, we must say it with him, either out loud or in silence, with great humility and devotion, just as if we had heard our Saviour say it and we were repeating it word for word after him.

St Albert: The giver of sanctity stands before the altar, with the heavenly Bread now confected, and encourages all present to desire this Bread. So our hope is placed in the kindness of our Lord, who by his own strength, though through the hands of the priest, breaks and distributes to each according to his need. At the beginning, mention is made of the *divine direction*, lest we be judged to ask rashly for something so great.

St Jerome: Our Lord so instructed his apostles that, daily at the sacrifice of his body, believers make bold to say, *Our Father, who art in heaven, hallowed be thy name*; they earnestly desire the name of God, which in itself is holy, to be hallowed in themselves. Then they say, *thy Kingdom come*, anticipating the hope of the future kingdom, and to this they couple the words, *thy will be done in earth as it is in Heaven* so that human weakness may imitate the angels, and the will of our Lord may be fulfilled on earth; the Apostles prayed for the *daily bread*, or the bread better than all food, that they might be worthy to receive the body of Christ. Next comes, *Forgive us our debts, as we also forgive our debtors*. No sooner do they rise from the baptismal font, and by being born again and incorporated into our Lord and Saviour thus fulfil what is written, *Blessed are they whose iniquities are forgiven and whose sins are covered*, than at the first communion of the body of Christ they say, *Forgive us our trespasses*, though these debts had been forgiven them at their confession of Christ. The bride, therefore, is washed, yet she cannot keep her purity, unless she be supported by the Lord.

St Thomas Aquinas: There are two ways in which we can forgive sins. The first is that of perfect men, when the one who has been wronged seeks to reconcile himself to the one who has wronged him. The second is within the scope of all, and is obligatory to all, that someone should grant pardon to one who asks it.

St Albert: But even if someone guards ill will towards the one who has wronged him, he should not be advised not to say the *Our Father*. Rather, let him say it in the person of the Church, who forgives the sins of all; and let him say it with groaning, that our Lord may soften his heart that he may forgive. For it often happens that in saying this very prayer, sinners are converted, and forgive that they may be forgiven.

St Augustine: When the saints pray, *Lead us not into temptation*, what else do they pray for than that they may persevere in their sanctity? Let the Church then observe her daily prayers: she prays that the unbelieving may believe, and therefore it is God who turns men to the faith; she prays that the believers may persevere, and so God gives them perseverance unto the end.

St Albert: Evil is either guilt or some punishment that will not lead to good. Against guilt already incurred, it is said, *Forgive us our trespasses*; against guilt that is feared, it is said, *Lead us not into temptation*; against punishments that will not lead to merit, comes the seventh petition, *But deliver us from evil*. So this last petition is made by the people, as if weak and afraid of punishment, to which the giver of sanctity quietly replies *Amen*, desiring that this be done before God, who alone knows the secrets of the heart.

Durandus: The *Amen* here signifies that our Lord will undoubtedly grant all these petitions, provided that we fulfil the final condition: *If you will forgive men their offences, your heavenly Father will forgive you also your offences.* But the priest speaks the *Amen* silently, for if he affirmed aloud that their prayer would be heard, it might seem to be presumption and ostentation.

Amalarius: The Lord's prayer, containing seven petitions, is recited in memory of the seventh day, when Christ rested in the tomb. On this day, the apostles were travailing in grief from fear of the Jews. And unless I am mistaken, they were praying to be delivered from evil, and obtained what they asked at the resurrection of their Lord. Holy Church also prays, as it were on the seventh day, and while the souls of the saints are now resting, she strives by fasting, watching, praying and charity, lest she be cut off by the dangers of this world from the hope of heavenly joys.

EMBOLISM

Deliver us, we beseech thee, O Lord, from all evils, past, present and to come; and by the intercession of the blessed and glorious Mary, ever a virgin, mother of God, together with thy blessed apostles Peter and Paul, and Andrew, and all the saints, graciously grant peace in our days: that by the help of thy mercy we may be always free from sin, and secure from all disturbance. Through the same Jesus Christ thy Son, our Lord, who with thee in the unity of the Holy Ghost liveth and reigneth, God, world without end.

St Thomas Aquinas: The people are prepared to receive communion first by a common prayer, the *Pater Noster*, and then by a private prayer offered for them by the priest, when he says, *Deliver us, we beseech thee.*

St Peter Damian: The silence that follows the *Our Father* represents the peace of our Lord's tomb, for on the Saturday, Christ rested in the tomb, according to the flesh. This prayer is called the Embolism, and it expounds the final petition of the *Our Father.*

Durandus: And yet Christ was not silent, for he who according to the flesh rested in the tomb, in the spirit descended into hell, that he might come upon the strong armed man, and in his greater strength overcome him. For this reason, the Roman Church recites this prayer aloud on Good Friday.

St Albert: *Deliver us, we beseech thee, O Lord, from all evils,* that is, from those that do not lead our weakness to something good and to greater merit; *past* when we incurred the guilt that we desire to be forgiven; *present,* in the pains that arise against us from the world; *and to come,* from temptations to unlawful deeds. And since he does not presume that this can be done without the support of the saints, he adds, *and by the intercession of the blessed and glorious virgin Mary,* who is a figure of the Church, and who as a mother conceives the sons of the Church in her chaste womb by her compassion, *the blessed apostles Peter and Paul,* the first of whom was the prince of the Church, and the other worked harder than all the rest, *and Andrew,* who brought Peter to Christ, and so was the apostle of the prince of the apostles.

Remigius: The Church asks for peace *in our days,* because after us others will pray in like manner, and after them others again, and so on till the end of time.

Durandus: Christ *sent forth the prisoners out of the pit, wherein is no water,* freeing them from *past, present and future evils,* and giving them perpetual peace, in which they will be forever *secure from disturbance.* So the priest asks that he and the whole Church may be delivered from this pit.

St Albert: When this is said, the priest takes the paten, which signifies the breadth of charity. And he kisses it, to show the charity which he has towards all.

Durandus: He makes the sign of the cross with the paten and kisses it, to show that if we have been reconciled to God the Father by the passion of the Son, we shall also be heirs of the kingdom of heaven.

St Peter Damian: The deacon and subdeacon bring the paten. They represent the holy women who with their hearts broadened by charity brought spices for ministering at the tomb. The priest accepts the paten, that is, Christ receives the heart made wide by charity. And since it was the Crucified whom they sought with such keen desire, the priest makes the sign of the cross with the paten upon himself; then he kisses it, to show that Christ forthwith fulfilled the women's desire, coming to meet them, and saying, *All hail.*

PATER · FILIUS · SPIRITUS SANCTUS

Fraction

*May the peace ✠ of
our Lord be ✠ always
✠ with you.*

St Peter Damian: The priest breaks the host so that we may recognize God in the breaking of bread, like those disciples in Emmaus.

St Albert: Those who were hungry had always sought this from Christ, for it is said in Lamentations, *The little ones have asked for bread, and there was none to break it for them.* The little ones are those who lived before Christ, who were weak for want of this breaking of Bread.

St Thomas Aquinas: The breaking of the host denotes three things. First, the division of Christ's body done in his passion.

St John Chrysostom: For although in the Eucharist one may see this done, yet on the cross not so, but the very contrary. For, *You shall not break a bone of him*, says one. But that which he suffered not on the cross, he suffers in the oblation for your sake, and submits to be broken, that he may fill all.

St Albert: Though our Lord's body itself is not broken, but rather the sacramental forms. For his body is whole and entire and perfect under every part.

St Vincent Ferrer: The host is divided into three parts, signifying that Christ was divided into three parts: his body was in the tomb, his blood was poured out upon the earth, and his soul was in Limbo.

St Thomas Aquinas: Secondly, the fraction denotes the various states of the mystical body.

St Albert: Now the breaking is to be done into three parts, since the mystical body which is incorporated into Christ is threefold. One part reigns triumphant with its Head, in heaven; one part still labours on earth; one part is in the pains of purgatory.

St Thomas Aquinas: Thirdly, the fraction denotes the distribution of graces proceeding from Christ's passion, as Dionysius says.

Dionysius: For Jesus, the supremely divine Word, who is one and simple and hidden, out of goodness and love towards man, came forth by his incarnation amongst us, to the compound and visible, and benevolently devised this unifying communion.

Durandus: It is also done to recall Christ's threefold condition. For first he dwelled among men, then he lay dead in the tomb, and now he lives eternally in heaven. Again it recalls the three who were present at Emmaus, that is, Christ and Cleophas, and, as some suppose, St Luke.

St Peter Damian: The deacon removes the pall, to show that *An angel of the Lord rolled back the stone* from the tomb. The priest makes the sign of the cross three times with the host above the chalice, since through the power of the Trinity, the soul of the Crucified returned to his flesh.

St Albert: He makes them over the chalice because the chalice signifies those who are still engaged in the warfare of this life, and it is these who most need peace.

Amalarius: He touches the four sides of the chalice with this fragment of the host, for by this Body the human race has been brought from the four winds to the unity of one body, and to the peace of the Catholic Church.

St Thomas Aquinas: The resurrection on the third day is represented by the three crosses that are made at the words, *May the peace of our Lord be always with you.*

Amalarius: By this peace we may understand that which was given to the just when Christ's soul descended into hell and drew thence all the faithful. Or again, we may understand it to refer to the peace that Christ's body knew when his soul returned to it.

Durandus: Thus, when the priest is about to say these words, as one who is to announce the good news of our Lord's resurrection, he takes hold of the paten once more. For *when the doors were shut, where the disciples were gathered together, for fear of the Jews, Jesus came and stood in the midst, and said to them: Peace be to you*, taking hold once more of his sheep who had fled in fear.

COMMINGLING

May this mingling and consecration of the body and blood of our Lord Jesus Christ be for those of us who receive it unto eternal life. Amen.

Durandus: A part of the host is put into the blood to show that one sacrament has been confected from the species of bread and wine.

Dom Guéranger: This rite is not one of the most ancient, although it is quite a thousand years old. Its object is to show, that, at the moment of our Lord's resurrection, his blood was reunited to his body, by flowing again in his veins as before.

St Paschasius: Or, the body and the blood are conjoined by this rite because the chalice represents the mystery of Christ's passion. For Christ's flesh and blood underwent the passion together.

St Thomas Aquinas: The chalice may represent both the passion of Christ, and the happiness of the blest, both of which are represented in this sacrament. In the first sense, the part of the host placed in the chalice represents those who are still sharers in the sufferings of

Christ; in the second, it represents those whose bodies are now fully blessed.

St Bonaventure: For one property of the chalice is that it is easy to receive, and in this respect it well symbolises the blessed, who enjoy their happiness without any hindrance.

St Albert: Pope Sergius[22] ordained that one part of the host be received by the one who stands at the altar in the person of Christ. This signifies that part of the mystical body which is in heaven, and has wholly passed into Christ. He ordained that the second part be put into the chalice, for the chalice signifies the suffering of this life, and so this denotes that part of the mystical body still labouring amid earthly pains. The third part he ordained to remain on the altar and to be received after the mysteries had been concluded, to denote those who are in the tombs, or in purgatory, and who in the end will be incorporated into Christ and live with him. But now that the devotion of Christ's faithful has diminished, and the altars are less frequented, the part that represents those in glory and the part that represents those in the tombs and those in purgatory awaiting with blessed hope their liberation from suffering are both received together by the priest.

St Thomas Aquinas: Or, the part placed in the chalice represents the body of Christ already risen, that is, Christ himself and the blessed Virgin, and any other saints who are already glorified in their bodies; the part

---

22. St Sergius I, who died in 701 AD.

that is eaten represents those still walking upon the earth, since it is those living upon the earth who use the sacraments; the part remaining on the altar to the end of Mass denotes the part of Christ's body lying in the tomb, since the bodies of the saints will be in the tombs until the end of the world, whether their souls are in heaven or in purgatory. And though one part of the host is no longer preserved to the end of Mass, to avoid danger, the symbolism of the three parts remains the same.

St Robert Bellarmine: Luther objects that mention is made of the commingling of Christ's body with his blood, when Christ is one and undivided. I reply that Catholics do not think that the body and the blood are commingled in their own nature, for they know that this could not be done unless Christ were again wounded, but rather with reference to the appearances of bread and wine. For just as he is said to be seen, touched and broken by reason of these species, so also is he said to be commingled.

St Alphonsus: This mingling of the holy species represents, too, the unity of divinity with humanity which was at first effected in the womb of Mary through the incarnation of the Word, and which is renewed in the souls of the faithful when they receive him in the eucharistic communion.

St Robert Bellarmine: Luther also objects that it is absurd to say that the consecration occurs by this commingling, when it has already been brought about by our Lord's words. But we do not ask that the consecration should now take place, but that the consecration that has already occurred may produce its effect. It can also perhaps be said that a new kind of consecration is here in question, which is now produced for the first time. For as something is said to be consecrated when it acquires a sacramental signification, so it is said to be consecrated again, when it acquires a new sacramental signification. So in this commingling a new consecration occurs, since the appearances that represented our Lord's death when they were apart, now, being joined together, represent his resurrection.

AGNUS DEI

Lamb of God, who takest away the sins of the world, have mercy on us. Lamb of God, who takest away the sins of the world, have mercy on us. Lamb of God, who takest away the sins of the world, grant us peace.

St Thomas Aquinas: As well as by prayer, the people are prepared for the communion by peace, which is conferred by the recitation of the *Agnus Dei*. For this is the sacrament of unity and peace.

Durandus: John the Baptist, seeing Jesus walking, said *Behold the Lamb of God, behold him who taketh away the sin of the world.* For Christ our pasch was immolated to take away sin. In the Old Testament, a lamb was offered for the sins of the people; but in the New Testament, Christ offered himself to God the Father. Rightly therefore, when the body and blood of our Lord is received, is the *Agnus Dei* sung, that we may all believe that this is the body and blood of that Lamb who took away the sins of the world by dying, and gave us eternal life by rising again.

St Albert: He is called 'the Lamb' because of his gentleness when suffering; and 'Lamb of God', because in his passion he was sacrificed to God. *I was as a meek* *lamb, that is carried to be a victim.* He is that *lamb who was slain* for all the elect *from the beginning of the world.* He is that lamb who was commanded to be immolated *in the morning and in the evening*: in the morning, in his members who preceded him; in the evening, in his own person and in those who belong to him and are offered to God since his coming.

St Robert Bellarmine: This prayer was introduced by Pope Sergius, more than nine hundred years ago.

St Peter Damian: After the resurrection, Christ immediately gave to the apostles the power of remitting sins. Therefore the choir now sings to him, *O Lamb of God, have mercy upon us.*

Amalarius: The prayer is made on behalf of those who are about to receive our Lord's body, that by the mercy of the innocent lamb, all sinful distractions of word and thought may be driven away, and that he who once took away sins from all the world may now take them from the Church, which is to receive him in the Eucharist.

St Albert: I think there is no other reason for saying *Lamb of God* thrice, than that the priest has already referred to a threefold evil. There is evil perpetrated, for which we must grieve, and evil put before us by temptation, which we must fear, and evil that prevents us from growing in merit, from which we request that all men may be delivered.

St Antoninus: Twice we seek mercy, asking that first our soul and then our body may be freed from misery. And a third time we say, *Agnus Dei,* seeking peace for both.

PAX

St Peter Damian: Lest we should speak of peace, but have it not in our hearts, Pope Innocent decreed that the kiss of peace should be given to all, and so it is.[23]

Remigius: The Church follows this practice by apostolic tradition: for the apostles frequently said to her, *Salute one another with a holy kiss.*

Origen: On account of this word, the custom was handed down in the Church that the brethren should welcome each other with this kiss after the Prayer.

Durandus: After our Lord had greeted the apostles, he said to them a second time, *Peace be to you*; and he breathed upon them and said, *Receive ye the Holy Ghost.* To symbolise this, after the priest has performed the commingling and prayed, he receives the peace from the Eucharist, whether from the very body of the Lord[24] or, according to others from his tomb, that is, from the chalice or from the altar, and bestows it upon the minister.

---

23. Pope Innocent I did not introduce the *Pax*, but defended the Roman custom of offering it after the prayers of the Canon, the practice to which Origen also alludes.
24. A practice that existed in the Middle Ages.

St Alphonsus: Before giving the peace, the priest kisses the altar to show that he cannot give peace unless he has first received it from Jesus Christ, who is represented by the altar.

St Innocent I: By the peace, it is clear that the people give their consent to all that has been done in the mysteries celebrated in the Church. This peace is the seal that shows that these mysteries have been accomplished.

St Cyril of Jerusalem: Think not that this kiss ranks with those given in public by common friends. It is not so: this kiss blends souls one with another, and solicits for them entire forgiveness. Therefore this kiss is the sign that our souls are blended together, and have banished all remembrance of wrongs.

Dionysius: For it is not possible to be gathered to the One and to partake of peaceful union with the One, when the people are divided among themselves.

Durandus: The people exchange this kiss, congratulating each other that through their Lord's death they have received his grace, and fellowship with the angels.

St Thomas Aquinas: But in Masses for the dead, when sacrifice is offered not for present peace but for repose for the dead, the *Pax* is omitted.

Dom Guéranger: For since the dead are no longer under the power of the keys of holy Church, she cannot give them peace; our relations with them are utterly changed.

PRIEST'S PREPARATION AND COMMUNION

St Robert Bellarmine: There follow three prayers before communion. The ancient order of Mass does not contain them; they have been brought in by the devotion of religious men.

Dom Guéranger: Those now found in the missal are not very ancient; nevertheless, they are at least a thousand years old.

St Albert: The priest prays, *Lord Jesus Christ, Son of the living God*, directing his eyes and his intention and his prayer to the one whom he holds in his hands, recalling the obedience with which he came to offer himself upon the altar of the Cross.

St Robert Bellarmine: Luther finds fault with the words, *Look not on my sins but on the faith of thy Church*, saying that the priests condemn themselves and declare that they receive unworthily. But two kinds of worthiness must be distinguished in speaking of this sacrament. The first is required of necessity and consists in this, that a man be not conscious of any mortal sin. The other kind would be required if we were to take into account only the excellence of the sacrament and not the weakness of the priest; namely, that we must be purer than the rays of the sun, and than the very angels. It is of this that priests speak when they declare themselves to be unworthy.

St Paschasius: Even if the one who offers is leprous, what is received is pure; for the body and blood of our Saviour cannot be defiled by any man's uncleanness.

St John Fisher: The priest, set over the mysteries as the hierarch, is the mediator between Christ and the people, and so he wears the likeness of each. Insofar as he consecrates and administers the sacrament, he acts as Christ; insofar as he receives it, he shares the lot of the poor people.

Dom Guéranger: The priest says, *May the body of our Lord Jesus Christ keep my soul into life eternal.* He speaks as if he were to communicate but once only in his life. One communion would of itself be sufficient to preserve our soul unto life eternal, for such is the intrinsic efficacy of this divine sacrament, provided for our wants by God.

St Alphonsus: This prayer recalls to our mind that this precious body and blood are given to us as a pledge of eternal life, and as a viaticum in order to pass from this exile to our heavenly country. Hence, when we receive Communion, we ought to be so disposed as if we had to leave the earth at once, to enter eternity.

ECCE, AGNUS DEI

Behold the Lamb of God: behold him who taketh away the sins of the world.

Lord, I am not worthy that thou shouldst enter under my roof: yet say but the word and my soul shall be healed.

Dionysius: This is the universal regulation of the divine mysteries, that the reverend leader should first partake and be filled with the gifts to be imparted through him from God, and so impart to others too.

St Thomas Aquinas: There are three reasons why it is for the priest to distribute holy communion. First, he consecrates in the person of Christ; and just as Christ consecrated his own body at the supper, so also he gave it to others to receive. Secondly, the priest has been set up as a mediator between God and the people; so just as it is for him to offer the people's gifts to God, so it is for him to give the divinely hallowed gifts to the people.

Thirdly, because from reverence for this sacrament, it is touched only by what has been consecrated; so just as the corporal and the chalice are consecrated, so are the hands of the priest.

St Leonard: It may be said with all truth that at every Mass, our Redeemer returns mystically to die for us, without really dying, at one and the same time really alive and as it were slain: *I saw a Lamb, standing as it were slain.*

St Vincent Ferrer: And just as a king sometime stands concealed behind a tapestry, but the soldiers believe that he is there and show reverence though they do not see him, so Christ, God and man, is within the tapestry of the host.

Origen: When you receive the holy food, that pure banquet; when you enjoy the bread and draught of life; when you eat and drink the body and blood of our Lord, then you receive him under your roof. And so you must humble yourself, imitating this centurion and saying, *Lord, I am not worthy that thou shouldst enter under my roof.*

St Robert Bellarmine: He strikes his breast at the words, *Lord, I am not worthy*. This ceremony expresses penitence, and is both natural and drawn from the gospel. For the publican struck his breast as he prayed, saying, *O God, be merciful to me a sinner.*

St John Fisher: Take away ceremonies from the Church, and you will straightaway destroy the worship of God among the greater part of Christians. Make sure that no one raises his hands, or bends his knee, or strikes his breast, or bares his head to pray, or stands to hear the gospel read, or does any similar thing, and you will see that within a few days, what we call devotion fades quite away. For the devotion which remains in the hearts of a few Christians, feeble spark of worship though it may be, is kept alive by ceremonies.

St John Chrysostom: Let us not, I pray you, let us not slay ourselves by our irreverence, but with all awe and purity draw nigh to it; and when you see it set before you, say to yourself, 'because of this body am I no longer earth and ashes, no longer a prisoner, but free: because of this I hope for heaven.'

St Augustine: Let no one eat that flesh, unless he has first adored it.

COMMUNION

May the body and blood of our Lord Jesus Christ preserve thy soul to life everlasting.

St Justin Martyr: We have learned that the food, made Eucharist by a word of prayer which comes from Jesus Christ, is by change the flesh and blood of the incarnate Jesus, from which our flesh and blood are nourished.

St John Fisher: The Father gave his Word veiled under the appearance of flesh, as man's Bread, by which they might be spiritually nourished by faith. Then Christ gave this same incarnate Word, that is, himself, covered by the appearance of bread, on which the apostles might feed, not only by faith, but in reality.

St Paschasius: Just as there was a tree of life in paradise, so the holy Church of God, which is called *the paradise of delights*, possesses in herself the mystery of life prefigured by that tree. And those who eat of it, keeping the commandments of life, cannot die for ever.

St John Chrysostom: Just as if someone were to put his hand or tongue into molten gold, and withdraw it, quite golden, so here, and in greater truth, those who share in the holy mysteries change their souls to gold.

St Peter Damian: Just as the widow of Sarephta ate daily, and yet the flour from her jar and the oil from her vessel were not lessened, so the universal Church daily receives but never consumes the flesh and blood of our Lord Jesus Christ.

St Thomas Aquinas: This sacrament foreshadows the enjoyment of God which will be in our heavenly home, and so it is called *eucharistia*, that is 'good grace', since *the grace of God is life everlasting*; or because it contains Christ, who is full of grace.

St Paschasius: It is distributed by none other than Christ, though the visible priest seems to be there, giving the sacrament to each.

Origen: Those who take part in the divine mysteries, when they come to receive our Lord's body, show great care and reverence, that not even a small part of it should fall to the ground, so that no part of the sacred gift be lost.

St John Chrysostom: A certain man once told me something that he had not learnt from a third party, but which he had himself seen and witnessed. At the point of going forth from this world, those who have shared in the holy mysteries with a pure conscience are put into the charge of angels, who escort them in this crossing over, for the sake of him whom they had received into their bodies.

St Isidore: Some say that unless sin prevents it, the

Eucharist should be received daily, since we ask for this as *our daily bread*, as our Lord commanded us. And they say well, if they receive it with piety and devotion and humility, not trusting in their own justice with proud presumption. But where such sins are found that separate a man from the altar as being, so to speak, dead, then first he must do penance; afterwards, let him receive this saving medicine.

St Albert: Some object to this, saying that our Lord after all showed himself to tax-collectors and sinners, for whom he had come. But they received him only outwardly, so as to be made ready to receive him inwardly. Again, he drew his body from sinners, such as Ahaz and Manasseh and Rahab the harlot, and others such, and did this for the sake of sinners; yet he never subjected his body to sin.

St Alphonsus: To eat worthily of this heavenly bread, we must be free from mortal sin, or at least be washed from it by the blood of the Lamb in the sacrament of penance. One should also be free from an actual affection for any venial sin to receive communion with greater effects.

St Augustine: If one man says that the Eucharist is not to be received daily, and another man that it is, let each do what according to his faith and devotion he believes that he should do. For Zacheus and the centurion did not quarrel among themselves, though one received our Lord with joy, and the other said, *I am not worthy that thou shouldst come under my roof*. Both honoured our Saviour, though not in the same way.

St Thomas Aquinas: And yet love and hope, to which Scripture always moves us, are to be preferred to fear; and so when Peter said, *Depart from me, for I am a sinful man, O Lord,* Jesus replied, *Fear not.*

Council of Trent: Some receive this holy sacrament only spiritually, namely those who eat this heavenly bread by desire, and with the living faith that *worketh through love.* And these receive its fruit and benefit.

Blessed Hyacinth Cormier: Thus did the blessed Virgin receive on the day of the Last Supper, as some say, and so she is called the foundress of spiritual communion.

ABLUTIONS

St Thomas Aquinas: Out of reverence for this sacrament, the priest takes wine after receiving it to wash his mouth, lest any of the sacrament remain. For like reason, he washes with wine the fingers with which he touched the body of Christ.

Durandus: It is not that he could have contracted any impurity by this contact, but rather he thus recalls his unworthiness, thinking himself unworthy to have celebrated so great a sacrament, according to the word of our Lord, *When you shall have done all these things that are commanded you, you say: We are unprofitable servants.*

St Albert; According to the custom of certain churches, the priest says, *May thy body, O Lord, which I have received, and the chalice that I have drunk cleave to my inmost parts,* not, that is, those of the body but those of the spirit. For the *inmost parts* are the understanding and will and reason and thoughts and desires of the soul.

Gabriel Biel: He covers the chalice,[25] as a sign that a

---

25. Biel is commenting on an earlier covering of the chalice, that which occurs at the end of the Canon. I have moved his remarks to suit the mystical interpretation of the priest's return to the epistle side.

day will come when the truth will be hidden, above all at the time of antichrist. And this was prefigured also in Isaiah, in the vision of the six-winged seraphim, who with two wings cover the Lord's face, and with two cover his feet, and with two fly. The head is the beginning, the feet are the end. And so in the beginning of the Church, before the coming of Christ, what would be revealed concerning him was veiled; and at the end, in the days of antichrist, the things to be believed and to be done will also be hidden, for deceitful error and wicked lust will hold sway.

COMMUNIO

St Thomas Aquinas: The celebration of Mass concludes by thanksgiving: the people rejoice at having received the mystery, which is signified by the chant after communion, and the priest offers thanks by prayer, just as Christ sang a hymn with the disciples when supper had been celebrated.

Durandus: This antiphon represents the joy of the apostles at Christ's resurrection, as it is said, *The disciples therefore were glad, when they saw the Lord.*

St John Chrysostom: *A hymn being said, they went out unto mount Olivet.* Some people in the celebration of the Mysteries do not wait for the last prayers, which represent our Saviour's prayer here. He gives thanks to God his Father before feeding his disciples, to teach us to begin our meals with thanksgiving; and he gives thanks afterwards and sings a hymn, so that we may learn to do the same.

Durandus: The priest went first to the right side of the altar, to show the gladness of our Lord's birth as man. When about to read the gospel, he went to the left hand, to suggest the sadness of the passion. But now again he returns to the right, that he may announce the joy of the resurrection.

St Antoninus: The two sides of the altar represent the two peoples. Since Christ came first to the Jews, the priest began the Mass at the right side. To read the gospel he went to the left side, for Christ passed by the preaching of the gospel to the Gentile nations. But he returns to the right side near the end of Mass, for the Jews, from whom the gospel faith has now passed, will at last be converted to Christ near the end of the world.

Durandus: And to whatever part of the altar the priest goes, the ministers follow behind him, showing the truth of our Lord's words, *If any man minister to me, let him follow me, and where I am, there also shall my minister be.*

POSTCOMMUNION

St Albert: After the communion chant, the priest turns to the altar with glad face and with hands apart and prays the prayer called the Postcommunion. It is so called because it seeks the perfection of communion. For what is received here beneath the veil that covers and hides it will be received openly in the beatitude of heaven.

Blessed Hyacinth Cormier: In the Postcommunion we renew, more or less, the intentions of the Secret, but now in the name of the sacrifice that has already been offered and the communion that has now been made.

St Alphonsus: The priest asks that through the merits of Jesus Christ in this mystery, and through the intercession of the saints whose memory is celebrated, this divine Saviour may always preserve him in this intimate union with him.

Durandus: The greeting that he offers before the prayer signifies that blessing which Christ is said to have given to his disciples, when he was about to ascend into heaven. For *he led them out as far as Bethany: and lifting up his hands, he blessed them. And it came to pass, whilst he blessed them, he departed from them, and was carried up* *to heaven.* The prayer itself represents the prayer of our Head, Jesus Christ, who intercedes for us daily before the Father.

Amalarius: So the priest turns back to the East, to entrust himself to our Lord's ascension.

Remigius: The *Amen* is the clear voice of the blood of Christ, making itself heard by the mouths of the faithful.

Blessed Hyacinth Cormier: The *Communio* and the Postcommunion are the start of our thanksgiving. This means giving to God something in exchange for what he has given us, to give to him the Eucharist of our lives by our daily actions, in return for the Eucharist that we have received at the altar of the Most High.

St Albert: Having finished the Postcommunion, the priest again turns to the people and says, *Dominus vobiscum*, desiring that when they depart from the temple they may not depart from our Lord. And the people again reply, *Et cum spiritu tuo*, for even after the Mass the giver of holiness must continue to perform spiritual works and not bodily ones for the sake of the people. And by this mutual salutation that indicates their communion, the Mass is accomplished.

ITE, MISSA EST

St Albert: When this is done, the deacon, or another in his place, cries out on festal days, *Ite, missa est*.

St John Fisher: Just as the ceremony of the paschal lamb, no simple matter, was called the *Phase*, which means 'the crossing', so the ceremony of consecrating the Eucharist is called *Missa*, 'the sending'. Some have supposed that the word means 'sending out' since the catechumens used to be sent out when the priest began the consecration of the sacred mysteries. Others claim that the word means a 'sending down', since the living victim is sent down to us from heaven by the Father. Others again have supposed *Missa* to mean 'sending across', since the prayers and oblations are sent across from the people to God through the priest, who plays the part of a mediator between them. Still others think that it comes from 'sending back', since when it is done, the people are sent back to their own homes.

St Antoninus: *Ite, Missa est*, which is understood: 'Go to your own homes, for the Mass is done'; or, 'the victim has been offered to God for the human race'; or, 'prayer has been sent to God for the people'; or, 'Go, follow Christ, do not mope in the world.'

Durandus: By saying this, the deacon represents what was said to the apostles, *This Jesus who was taken up from you into heaven.*

Amalarius: O that having heard from the deacon, *Ite, Missa est,* our mind might follow to that heavenly country where our Head has preceded us! For thus, by desire, we shall be where the desired of all the nations now awaits us.

St Robert Bellarmine: At Masses of Advent and Lent, it is said, not *Ite, Missa est,* but *Let us bless our Lord.* This is simply done to express the more severe character of these seasons; for it seems somehow to be rather mournful, that the dismissal is not public, but rather each one departs by himself.

Dom Guéranger: The faithful are not dismissed during these days of expiation, because it is supposed that they would like to remain longer in prayer.

Amalarius: Holy Church says *Deo gratias,* according to the apostolic example. For when the apostles had adored Jesus, they *went back into Jerusalem with great joy.*

Durandus: The end of the Mass represents the end of the world. And so *Ite, missa est,* or *Let us bless our Lord,* represent the freedom which will be granted to the just in their homeland, where they will bless God forever.

AFTER THE END

Dom Guéranger: The priest kisses the altar, raises his eyes to heaven, stretches out his hands, and then bows before the Cross, saying, *May almighty God bless you,* then turning round to the people, he adds, blessing them: *the Father and the Son and the Holy Spirit;* to which they answer: *Amen.*

Blessed Hyacinth Cormier: The last kiss, before the final blessing, is a kiss of gratitude, for all the benefits received in the course of the celebration.

Durandus: This last blessing over the people represents the sending of the Holy Spirit, whom our Lord sent upon the apostles after he had ascended into heaven, according to his promise, *You shall receive the power of the Holy Ghost coming upon you.* It also recalls the last blessing that will be given when Christ says, *Come, ye blessed of my Father, possess you the kingdom prepared for you from the foundation of the world.*

St Francis de Sales: At the blessing, we should think that Jesus Christ is at that moment giving us his own blessing.

St Vincent Ferrer: For this blessing has a great power from Christ who is present.

Dom Guéranger: The blessing having been given, the priest goes to the gospel side of the altar, and there reads the beginning of the gospel according to St John. The custom originates from the Middle Ages. At that period, as in earlier times also, the faithful had a great devotion to the having a portion of the gospel read over them, and the commencement of that of St John was a special favourite. To simplify the matter, it was decided to recite it over all those assembled, at the end of the Mass. The devotion of the faithful, therefore, alone originated this addition.

St Augustine: A certain philosopher once said, that the beginning of this gospel ought to be inscribed in letters of gold, and set up in the most prominent place in every church.

Gloss: It may be said that the reading of this gospel, represents the apostles' message spreading through the world by the power of the Holy Spirit.

Durandus: And going out of the people's sight he enters the place where he vested: for when Christ ascended into heaven, the clouds took him from the sight of those who gazed thereon . . .

Saints, *Beati*, and other ecclesiastical authors cited, and principal sources used

St Clement of Rome (1st century) Early successor of St Peter. His *Letter to the Corinthians* contains some of the earliest references to the formal prayer or liturgy of the Church.

St Justin Martyr (c.100-165) Lay apologist. His *First Apology* briefly describes the ceremonies of the Eucharistic liturgy.

Origen (c.185-254) Theologian and priest. He was a native of Alexandria, whose Church had been founded by St Mark, the disciple of St Peter.

St Cyprian (d.258) Bishop of Carthage and martyr. His *Letter to Caecilius* insists on the importance of retaining the liturgical customs received from Christ through the apostles.

St Cyril of Jerusalem (c.315-87) Bishop of Jerusalem. His *Mystagogic Catecheses* describe how the Eucharistic sacrifice was performed in that see.

St Basil (c.330-79) Bishop of Caesarea in Asia Minor and doctor of the Church. His work *On the Holy Spirit* explains how the Church follows by apostolic tradition many customs relating to the sacred liturgy.

St Gregory of Nyssa (c.330-c.395) Bishop of Nyssa in Asia Minor and brother of St Basil.

St Ambrose (c.339-397) Bishop of Milan and doctor of the Church. His work *On the Sacraments* contains the central prayers of the Roman Canon.

St Jerome (c.345-420) Translator of the Bible, priest and doctor of the Church.

St John Chrysostom (c.347-407) Bishop of Constantinople and doctor of the Church. His *Homilies* contain many references to the awesome nature of the Eucharistic liturgy.

St Augustine (354-430) Bishop of Hippo in North Africa and doctor of the Church. In his work *On baptism against the Donatists*, he notes that customs followed by the whole Church and not introduced by a general council must be of apostolic institution.

St Innocent I (d.417) Pope from 402 AD. His *Letter to Decentius* states that the Churches of the West must follow the rite of Rome, bequeathed to that Church by St Peter.

St John Cassian[26] (c.360-after 430). Disciple of St John Chrysostom and monastic founder.

St Germanus of Paris (c.496-576) Bishop of Paris. A short commentary on the rite of Mass used in that church is ascribed to him.

St Gregory the Great (c.540-604) Benedictine monk, pope and doctor of the Church. To him is attributed the perfecting of the Roman Canon.

St Isidore (c.560-636) Bishop of Seville and doctor of the Church. His encyclopaedic *Etymologies* contains a

---

26. He is so styled in the *Catechism of the Catholic Church*.

treatise 'On Ecclesiastical Offices'.

St Bede (c.673-735) Benedictine monk, priest and the only English doctor of the Church. His *Ecclesiastical History* records how the Roman rite was re-established on English soil.

Blessed Alcuin of York (c.740-804) Abbot. The sole quotation by which he is represented in this work is drawn from a letter to the Emperor Charlemagne.

Amalarius (c.780-850/1) Pupil of Alcuin and Bishop of Metz. His work *On Ecclesiastical Offices* contains a detailed mystical commentary on the ceremonies of the Roman Mass.

St Paschasius Radbertus (c.790-860) Benedictine abbot. His book *On the Body and Blood of our Lord* is the first doctrinal monograph on the Holy Eucharist, and is illustrated by many references to the Roman rite.

Walafrid Strabo (c.808-49) Benedictine abbot. His work *On the origin and development of ecclesiastical things*, shows a strong sense of the necessity and value of liturgical development.

Remigius of Auxerre (c.841-908) Benedictine monk. He taught St Odo, the great abbot of Cluny, and a short but beautiful *Exposition of the Mass* is ascribed to him.

St Peter Damian (1002-72) Monk and doctor of the Church. An *Exposition of the Canon of the Mass* is included among his works.

St Anselm (1033-1109) Benedictine monk, Archbishop of Canterbury and doctor of the Church. His

Letter to Bishop Walerannus discusses some disputed liturgical questions.

Blessed Isaac of Stella (c.1100-c.1178) Cistercian monk. Originally from Northumbria, his *Letter on the Office of the Mass* is a dense, mystical commentary on the central prayers of the Roman Canon.

St Albert (before 1200-1280) Dominican friar, Bishop of Regensburg and doctor of the Church. His work *On the Sacrifice of the Mass* offers a literal and mystical commentary on the entire rite; another work, *On the Eucharist*, considers the nature of the sacrament.

St Bonaventure (c.1217-74) Franciscan friar, cardinal and doctor of the Church. An *Exposition of the Mass* is included among his works.

St Thomas Aquinas (c.1225-74) Dominican friar and doctor of the Church. His *Summa Theologiae* and *Scriptum on the Sentences of Peter Lombard* contain succinct literal and mystical explanations of the ceremonies of the Mass.

Durandus (c.1230-96) Bishop of Mende in France. His vast *Rational of Divine Offices* was described by Prosper Guéranger as 'the last word of the Middle Ages on the mystical meaning of the divine cult'.

St Vincent Ferrer (1350-1413) Dominican friar. The sermons of this popular preacher and thaumaturge contain much instruction about participation in the Mass.

St Antoninus (1389-1459) Dominican friar and Archbishop of Florence. His *Summa Theologica* discusses the fruits of the Eucharistic sacrifice and the meaning of its ceremonies.

Gabriel Biel (c.1420-95) Professor at Tubingen and 'Brother of the Common Life'. His *Exposition of the Canon of the Mass* is strongly influenced by St Albert's commentary.

St John Fisher (1460-1535) Bishop of Rochester and martyr. Many of his writings defend the sacrifice of the Mass and the existence within the Church of a true priesthood.

Ven. Louis of Granada (1504-88) Dominican friar. A popular and prolific spiritual writer, whom St Teresa of Avila described as 'a man given to the world by God for the great and universal good of souls.'

St Robert Bellarmine (1542-1621) Jesuit, cardinal and doctor of the Church. His *Controversies* are a monumental Catholic response to the objections of the Protestant Reformers.

St Lawrence of Brindisi (1559-1619) Capuchin friar and doctor of the Church. A polyglot and popular preacher, he was said to know the whole text of the bible in its original languages.

St Francis de Sales (1567-1622) Bishop of Geneva and doctor of the Church. He wrote a short treatise for lay people on participation in the holy sacrifice; unfortunately his work *The Catholic Controversy* does not treat of the rite of Mass in any detail.

St Leonard of Port Maurice (1676-1751). Franciscan friar. An outstanding popular preacher, his work *The*

Hidden Treasure: Holy Mass is addressed both to priests and lay people.

St Alphonsus Liguori (1696-1787) Bishop of 'St Agatha of the Goths', founder of the Redemptorists and doctor of the Church. As well as a detailed treatment of liturgical law in his *Theologia Moralis*, he explains the ceremonies of the Mass in the work *The Sacrifice of Jesus Christ*.

Ven. John Henry Newman (1801-1890) Cardinal and founder of the English Oratory. Perhaps the finest mind ever to have adorned the English Church, his novel *Loss and Gain* contains a vivid description of the Mass as experienced by a convert.

Dom Prosper Guéranger (1805-75) Benedictine abbot and re-founder of Solesmes. He gave his life to promote the worthy celebration of the sacred liturgy; his works include *Liturgical Institutions*, *The Liturgical Year* and *The Holy Mass*. The cause for his beatification has recently been opened.

Blessed Hyacinth Cormier (1832-1916) Dominican friar and Master-General. He did much to restore the primitive fervour of the Order, and among many other works wrote the historical and devotional study, *The Dominican Liturgy*.

Blessed Columba Marmion (1858-1923) Benedictine abbot. Of Irish birth, he entered religious life in Maredsous in Belgium. His spiritual conferences, published in various books, seamlessly unite monastic tradition and theological science.

Blessed John XXIII (1881-1963) Pope from 1958. He placed St Joseph's name in the Roman Canon, and insisted in the encyclical *Veterum Sapientia* on the primary place to be given to the Latin language in the life of the Church.

Paul VI (1897-1978) Pope from 1963. He strongly upheld the Church's Eucharistic faith in the encyclical *Mysterium Fidei*, and insisted on the value of Latin chant in the Apostolic Letter, *Sacrificium Laudis*. He also promulgated various liturgical books containing new liturgical forms.

Dionysius *(Date disputed)* The modern scholarly consensus holds that this mystical theologian used the writings of the pagan Proclus (410/12-485), and so assigns to him a date at the end of the 5th or the start of the 6th century. However, Dionysius' 19th century translator, the Puseyite John Parker, argues that it was Proclus who borrowed from the Christian writer, and defends the traditional 1st century date.

BIBLIOGRAPHY

This is not a complete list of sources. It lists the works from which I have quoted most often, and other works which treat of liturgical matters directly rather than in passing, and which require more detailed references than were given in the preceding biographical notes.

Dionysius: *De Ecclesiastica Hierarchia*, P.G. 3, 369-584.

St Cyprian: *Ad Caecilium*, P.L. 4, 372-89.

St Augustine: *Letters*, vol.1, 54, 'To Januarius', tr. Parsons, New York 1954.

St Innocent I: *Ad Decentium*, P.L. 20:551-561.

St Germanus: *Expositio brevis antiquae liturgiae gallicanae*, P.L. 72, 89-94.

St Gregory the Great: *Ad Ioannem*, P.L. 77, 955-8.

St Isidore of Seville: *De ecclesiasticis officiis,* P.L. 83, 737-826.

Blessed Alcuin of York: *Ad Carolum magnum*, P.L. 100, 431-7.

Amalarius of Metz: *De ecclesiasticis officiis libri iv,* P.L. 105, 985-1242; *Eclogae de Officio Missae*, P.L. 105, 1313-32.

St Paschasius Radbertus: *De corpore et sanguine Domini*, CCCM 16.

Walafrid Strabo: *De ecclesiasticarum rerum exordiis et incrementis*, P.L. 114, 919-966.

Remigius of Auxerre: *De celebratione Missae*, P.L. 101, 1246-71.

St Peter Damian: *Expositio canonis Missae*, P.L. 145, 880-91.

St Anselm: *Ad Walerannum episcopum*, P.L. 158, 547-552.

Blessed Isaac of Stella: *Ad Ioannem episcopum*, P.L. 194, 1889-1896.

St Albert the Great: *Opera Omnia*, ed. Borgnet, 1899, vol. 38, *De Sacrificio Missae* and *De Eucharistia*.

St Bonaventure: *Opera Omnia*, Quaracchi, 1898, vol. 8, *De Praeparatione ad Missam*, pp. 99-106.

St Thomas Aquinas, *Summa Theologiae*, IIIa, q. 83; *Scriptum super Sententias*, IV dist. 1, 8, 12-3, 15.

William Durandus: *Rationale divinorum officiorum*, Book 4, CCCM 140.

St Vincent Ferrer: *Omnia Opera*, Valencia, 1693, *Sermones*, vol. I-III, *passim*.

St Antoninus: *Summa Theologica, Pars Tertia, titulus* 13, c.5-6; *titulus* 14, c.4-5, 12.

St Robert Bellarmine: *Omnia Opera*, ed. Fèvre, 1873, *Controversia* 10, lib.6.

St Francis de Sales, *Œuvres Complètes*, Paris, 1821, vol. 14, pp. 475-6, 501-2.

Prosper Guéranger: *La Sainte Messe*, Solesmes, 1885.

P.G. – *Patrologia Graeca*
P.L. – *Patrologia Latina*
CCCM – *Corpus Christianorum: Continuatio Mediaevalis*